The Sixth COMMANDMENT

GOD, MY ABORTION AND ME

F I R S T   E D I T I O N
Published in 2019

Written by: Rhonda Lobosco | RhondaLobosco@comcast.net | www.Facebook.com/Rhonda Lobosco

ISBN: 978-0-578-57703-6

Category: Christian Living, Abortion

Library of Congress Cataloging-in-Publication Data

Cover Design & Formatting by: Eli Blyden | www.EliTheBookGuy.com

Published & Printed in the United States of America | Tampa, Florida

Disclaimer

This book details the author's personal experiences and opinions with and about emotional intelligence. The author is not a licensed psychologist. Except as specifically stated in this book, neither the author or publisher, nor authors, contributors or other representatives will be liable for damages arising out of or in connection with the use of this book. You understand that this book is not intended as a substitute for consultation with a licensed legal or accounting professional. Before you begin any change in your lifestyle in any way, you will consult a licensed professional to ensure you are doing what is best for your situation. This book provides content related to emotional intelligence topics. As such, use of this book implies your acceptance of this disclaimer.

Special Thanks

Thank you to my friend Jesus. I shared my most shameful secret with Him and He created a way to complete healing, when I thought there was no way. He gently revealed how to accept His forgiveness through His Word, prayer, and fasting. Jesus imparted a spiritual understanding and path to forgiving myself so that I could live courageously through Him and for Him. My God is awesome!

Thank you to my best friend and husband, Jimmie Lobosco, whom I love with all my heart. He is a man of integrity and steadfast commitment to Jesus, me and the vows we lovingly spoke to each other almost 20 years ago. Jesus placed us together when we were yet sinners. He foresaw our potential in Him by tenderly guiding and speaking truth to our hearts. Jimmie sees God all around him. Whether it be the Garden of Eden he has created in our backyard, or the thoughtful care and love he lavishes on our four-legged family members: Sophie, Skipper, and Peaches. Jimmie is my rock and I cherish our marriage, friendship, and walk with God. I'm excited to see what God has planned for him and us.

Thank you to my mom, Betty Friston, for her lovingkindness. Throughout my life, she has never said an unkind word to me. I'm sure she endured unspeakable heartache in my early years trying to protect my brother and me. She epitomizes the definition of unconditional, motherly love through her actions, words, and gentle caresses on the forehead. I love her very much and our walk with God has been one of the greatest blessings of my life.

Thank you to my kind and compassionate friend and counselor at the Pregnancy Resource Center in Lodi, California (aka Directions Medical Clinic). She guided me through the 10-week

Christian-based Post-Abortion Bible study that prepared the foundation for the journey that Jesus and I embarked upon. She is a woman of faith and commitment to Jesus Christ and I have great respect and love for her.

Thank you to John Barron for taking the time and care to edit my manuscript. He is thoughtful, kind, and brimming with humorous insights. He is a man of God and walks the walk. I cherish our friendship and look forward to many more years sitting next to him and his sweet and godly wife, Kathy, on the pew at Christian Life Center.

Thank you to my friend Suzanne Franco. She has been my greatest cheerleader. Suzanne has encouraged me to share my unique testimony because she could see healing encircling my story. Suzanne has been a witness to my spiritual journey, all the while, laughing, crying, and singing, "I Can Only Imagine" at the top of our lungs.

Thank you to Eli Blyden who thoughtfully listened to my story and masterfully designed a book cover that honors the vision Jesus gave me. He is talented, kind, sensitive, and witty. Eli gently guided me through the unknown waters of my first writing endeavor. I am grateful for our friendship.

Table of Contents

The Sixth COMMANDMENT

GOD, MY ABORTION AND ME

*Healing for those who have,
and guidance for those who haven't*

BY RHONDA LOBOSCO

CHAPTER ONE

Wooden Pew

My story begins around 1964 on a wooden pew at the First Pentecostal Church in Modesto, California. I was four years old.

Sunday morning service was the highlight of the week for a faithful church-going family. I was raised to dress in a respectful manner to honor the Lord and as a small child, Sunday best meant Mom donning me in a black velvet dress with a delicate white lace collar, white tights with ruffles on the bottom, and black patent-leather shoes with shiny silver buckles. My thick wavy jet-black hair trailed down the back of my neck forming a soft question mark. I recognize how foretelling this subtle physical display was as I have questioned all things throughout my life.

Church life dominated our lives and we regularly fellow-shipped with grandparents, aunts, uncles, cousins, and church friends, attending twice on Sunday and several nights during the week. The lifestyle protected us from the outside world as the Bible states, "Therefore come out from among them And be separate, says the Lord. Do not touch what is unclean, And I will receive you." (2 Corinthians 6:17 NKJV). The Lord began methodically constructing my foundation and sheltering me during those early years in preparation for the calamitous journey which soon revealed itself through my choices, ultimately leading to decades of trials and suffering.

During my time of shelter, a wonderful memory is me standing on a wooden pew, dancing, clapping my hands, stomping my feet, and swaying to the music as Mom sang and played the accordion, while the choir erupted into harmonious song and the congregation followed. Fifty-four years later, I lovingly reminisce on the power of a church filled with God-loving people singing old gospel songs. These carefree, joyful moments formed the cornerstone of faith for the little girl dancing on the wooden pew.

My maternal grandparents loved Jesus Christ so much that I still hear stories of their love, kindness, and steadfast commitment to the youth ministry. People say, "I can still see Brother Holliday leading the choir. . .he sure loved those old church hymns." Grandpa Bill, or PoPo Bill to me, was a youth minister, and during Mom's early years, there were many young men who frequented their home, yearning to hear the gospel, sing, and study God's Word. My roots are not only spiritual but musical as PoPo Bill played the guitar, Uncle Sheril the trumpet, Aunt Carolyn the piano, and Mom the accordion. Gospel hymns were sung, scriptures shared, and Grandma Bertie's gift was preparing a bounty of homemade biscuits and gravy, fried chicken, or fresh catfish caught that day in the Stanislaus River. The food fed their bodies, and the scriptures and fellowship fed many lonely souls as PoPo Bill was, in some cases, their only father figure.

My father was one of these young men longing for acceptance and love. He immersed himself in the gospel and became a street minister. He and a few of the fellas would pile into a powder blue '56 Pontiac, drive to skid row and stand on street corners outside of bars preaching and thumping their bibles to anyone who would listen, while Mom stood behind playing the accordion and singing hymns with the gals. Dad's scripture reads, "Then Peter said to them, 'Repent, and let every one of you be baptized in the name of

Jesus Christ for the remission of sins; and you shall receive the gift of the Holy Spirit.'" (Acts 2:38 NKJV).

Dad's family rejected church life and he was not raised to believe or understand the values of love and compassion Jesus taught. His house was filled with sex, violence, lies, and betrayal, and he never shared one story of love or compassion about his childhood; not one, ever. Dad's transformation from sinner to saint must have been thrilling, inspiring, and hopeful. . .until it wasn't.

CHAPTER TWO

The Old White Bus

I was six years old when we moved to Stockton, California. My parents sent my brother and me to church, yet they didn't attend, as something happened during those years. Their abrupt departure from church life was likely prompted by a haunting memory that took me decades to unravel.

We often visited Grandma Bertie in Modesto and on the return trip, sitting in the backseat of the car, I was gently lulled by the low murmur of the engine and the whoosh of rows of sweet summer corn, fragrant peach orchards, and lush alfalfa fields swiftly passing by. My pigtailed hair whipped around my face as I leaned my head against the cool window frame. A few of the light brown strands loosed from the rubber bands and clung to my eyelashes. As we merged off the highway toward home, I gently brushed them away with my hand as my eyes fell upon the flashing bright blue fluorescent light of the Blue Light Motel. The blue fluorescent light blazing in the evening sky was flashing an eerie signal in Morse code. As the car rounded the corner of the off ramp, my eyes followed and my head turned toward the bright blue fluorescent light. I am mysteriously connected to this place but I don't know why.

Three years prior, Dad wandered away from God as Mom soon discovered his infidelities. The deep betrayal Mom must have felt spurred the events which lead to our enslavement. Dad fearing that Mom would leave, raced to my grandmother's house, grabbed my infant brother and me and put us in the backseat of the car, speeding away as Mom frantically followed the red tail lights. She stopped abruptly, wild eyes stayed on the back of the car, watching as it flew over the railroad tracks racing to beat an oncoming train. We were crying and calling for our mother, but Dad was determined to teach Mom a lesson that would systematically imprison us for the next 14 years.

He held us captive in the Blue Light Motel. It was a typical cheap highway motel; dark and dreary and frightening for a child yearning for the comfort of her mother. We returned home on the third day after an agreement had been made between my parents. Some agreements require a signature or a notary to verify the signatories. This agreement was more binding than any legal document. The terms were quite clear: if Mom left Dad, he would take us and she would never see us again. Most agreements can be nullified if you have a clever attorney, but the consequences of breaking this agreement would threaten the lives of my brother and me; therefore, Mom remained and protected us the best she could. This was during the early 60's and shelters, financial assistance, counseling, and the plethora of programs our country offers today were not available. Marriage meant, "You've made your bed, now lie in it."

Of course, it took years for the fullness of this memory to emerge, but in the meantime, every Sunday morning the old white bus emblazoned with First Pentecostal Church in big broad black letters pulled up in front of the house. My brother and I would awake early, put on our finest clothes, and fidget on the couch with ears cocked for the loud squeak of the brakes immediately followed by a "honk, honk." We'd run out the door, excited and happy, racing up the steps and quickly find a seat with friends whose parents did not attend church either. I recall the bus being hot in the summer and cold in the winter; the windows jammed halfway up and the heater working some of the time. Occasionally, a broken spring on the faded vinyl seat pinched the back of my leg and I'd cry out momentarily as I jumped up and down. We were young and had a modest upbringing and these minor drawbacks didn't faze us. We cheerfully sang to and from church, clapping our hands and stomping our feet to, "When You're Happy and You Know It."

Since church consumed our lives early on, we never questioned whether we'd go on Sunday any more than we'd question school on Monday. The scriptures I learned, and the care and love of my Sunday School teachers implanted a seed in my soul. The seed would lay dormant for decades, but the teachings of Jesus and joyful memories of Sunday School kept me tethered to God waiting for the moment to sprout. A seed needs a cool dark place to germinate, and my heart, which would soon turn dark and cold, was the perfect place to bury those wonderful memories.

Life started changing when I was about ten years old as the atmosphere in our home became unrecognizable from the church-filled years. Childhood rebellion within me took a foothold. Rebellion is like a smoldering fire in a furnace, and when fueled, ignites and devours everything within its reach. My fire was fueled by thoughts of unfairness.

Sunday mornings began with small acts of rebellion. Why should I have to go to church if my parents didn't? I lay in bed listening to Mom shouting at me to get up. I didn't want to get dressed and this small act of disobedience quickly escalated. I learned very early that I had more stamina than my parents and could hold out much longer. Eventually, I beat them down because they couldn't come up with an argument I would accept, or they could believe. I started sleeping in, the bus stopped pulling up in front of the house, and I no longer heard the loud squeak of the brakes or the "honk, honk" that sent my brother and me racing out the front door and up the bus steps. I look back and see this is the moment my life started taking a turn. It began as a small turn off course, not enough to notice, just a few degrees to the right, as if someone gently placed their hand under my chin and slightly turned my head. My head turned just enough for my eyes to gaze upon a new world I had not seen before and my thoughts and actions quickly followed.

CHAPTER THREE

The Drink

A t first glance, the turn was so subtle I didn't see a change in my life. Mom still woke me up for school and had breakfast ready and lunch packed in my Snoopy lunch box. I was a good student and top of my class in reading, a member of the safety patrol, competitive at tetherball, and played catcher and first base on the girls' softball team. I wasn't missing anything because everyone I knew was doing the same thing. Our family had become distracted by the new direction and it was easy for us to veer away from the church lifestyle as we naturally progressed down an unknowing disastrous path.

There were about 60 kids on our block and we all played and fought together. We had sleepovers, built forts, played tag football, and rode Stingray bikes to Thrifty Drug Store for a scoop of rainbow sherbet on a sugar cone. On those warm summer evenings, we stayed outside until Mom called out the front door telling us to come in when the streetlight came on. I rarely wore shoes during those months and when September came, my wide feet didn't fit into my new school shoes.

My life appeared normal, and there were many days it was, but I harbored a secret I couldn't share with anyone. I couldn't share it because I was sure I was the only one feeling this way and who would believe me. Many times, I didn't want to believe it myself; I wanted it to be a dream I could awake from.

I was sure other kid's dad didn't say things to their little girl that my dad said to me, such as, "I wouldn't have to cheat on your mom if you were nicer to me." I had no idea what that meant, so I made him a fried bologna sandwich on toasted bread. I was sure other kid's dad didn't tell them to bend over and grab their ankles as he ripped the silver-rivetted belt from his pants, reared back, and hit their buttocks and back of their legs hard enough to leave welts. I was sure other kid's dad didn't start arguments with their mom so they could escape to their girlfriend's house. This couldn't be happening in other kid's houses because I didn't see it. I didn't want my friends to spend the night with me, but I couldn't wait to stay with them. My secret stayed buried with me and shame took up refuge along with rebellion. Rebellion and shame became my constant companions and my motivation for decisions I made for years to come.

I was about 12 years old and during the hot summer months in the San Joaquin Valley, the family traveled to New Hogan Lake for a Saturday filled with water-skiing, playing Marco Polo with my brother in the cool lake water, and binging on Fig Newtons, potato chips, and soda. I loved these weekends and I have fond memories of those days, until I didn't anymore. I didn't know it yet, but I was about to witness my father's infidelities up close.

Our neighbors and their two small children were invited to spend a day on the lake. I was just learning to water ski and was excited to have my dad pull me around the lake. I wanted him to see how well I was doing under his direction because I wanted him to be proud of me.

Boating laws require a spotter, someone who is assigned to watch the skier, and the spotter was the neighbor woman with Dad at the helm. I excitedly jumped into the water and quickly put on my double skis as the boat rounded me and the 75' rope circled behind. I reached over my head, clutched the double handle, and placed the ropes around my skis for stabilization, just how Dad taught. When I was balanced and ready, I did a thumbs up and, because I was so skinny, popped up, skis skimming across the glasslike water. I'm feeling so proud of myself and excited that I got up on the first try. Dad was looking over his shoulder and smiling, as the cool breeze and misty water cascaded over my face. I'm building up courage to cross the wake because this is a scary moment for a new skier, but I held tight, keeping my skis together and successfully crossed over. Dad was raising his hand victoriously and followed with a big smile and I'm feeling so good about myself and really loving him at that moment.

Then, I see the woman's hand reach over and caress Dad's back. What is happening up there? The sun is in my eyes, but I'm sure of what I saw. I'm startled and can't look away because my vision is captive to the circumstances and I must look forward at the boat to keep my balance and concentration. I'm not very confident and a bit shaky and I can't believe what I'm seeing. They start rubbing their hands all over each other, in places I am too young to know about, and I'm watching. I want to vomit, but I can't because I'll fall into the water and I don't want anyone on shore to ask questions. I'm frozen in time and I know this memory is going to change who I could have been. They are caressing, laughing, and looking back at me. How could Dad do this. This was our moment where I could show him all he taught me and it's been replaced with a memory of sickness, pain, and disgust. I'm crying so hard while trying to keep my balance, although I should just let go and allow the water to pour over my face and wash the tears from my eyes. I hold onto the rope and he swings the boat around in front of the beach as I let go and glide to the shore. Everyone on shore is clapping and shouting. It was a perfect run all the way to the beach, except for the eye-witness account of virtual molestation that just occurred.

The onlookers on shore had no idea that a beautiful memory had just been crushed by the father I loved, yet was growing to hate. I gather my skis and walk up toward the beach and sit on a towel. I'm in a state of shock and don't know how to handle what I just saw. I can't look at my mother. I'm not sure what I'm feeling, but something tells me to keep his secret.

During the 70's, house parties were the rage and my parents participated in several with their neighbors. Saturday nights were reserved for dancing and drinking until early morning. I was 13 years old and my parents hosted a party in the garage. I remember lying in bed and being magically drawn to the music of "Midnight Train to Georgia" and "Night Fever" in the distance. I snuck quietly down the hallway in my pink flannel nightgown, sliding low against the wall, hoping to get a peek at the action. Mom quickly shuffled me back to the safety of my bedroom, tucking me in, and softly kissing my forehead. I recall listening to the music as it flowed throughout the house, wave after wave, gently rocking me to sleep.

The following morning, while my parents were sleeping, I snuck into the garage to eat some leftover snacks and peruse the record collection. While rummaging through the stale potato chips and warm French onion dip, I found a cocktail. I knew it was wrong to take a drink, but my parents were sleeping and no one would know. I picked up the plastic cocktail glass half-filled with a brown diluted liquid and held it to my nose. I took a long whiff and a strong alcohol smell burst into my nostrils and made my stomach tumble. I slyly took a sip and instantly coughed and gagged. The liquor tasted strong and bitter and immediately the top of my head became light and floaty, and a relaxed feeling flowed through my body and warmed me inside. . .a comfort.

Just a few years before when I turned my head in another direction and began traveling with my companions; rebellion and shame, I recognized I needed something to keep me warm on my journey. Along the way, I picked up a blanket of sadness and loneliness. The blanket kept me warm on the outside, but I needed solace on the inside. In those early morning hours, when I snuck into the garage, I found something that warmed me on the inside. I found an inner comfort in alcohol and thus birthed my journey into alcoholism.

At 15 years old, the pressure was building in the house as Dad's risky behavior escalated. On another occasion, while Mom was at work, he snuck out of the house, hopped on his motorcycle on his way to the same girlfriend's house. I sensed where he was headed because he had a pathetic pattern of behavior, similar to a tell in poker. A tell is a change in a player's behavior that gives clues to that player's hand. A player gains an advantage if they observe and understand the meaning of another player's tell, particularly if the tell is unconscious and reliable. Dad was so deep in his behavior that he was unaware of his tell, but I had years of experience watching and waiting for it to appear.

I was an inexperienced, unlicensed driver behind the wheel of three-quarter ton Chevrolet pickup, but my rage and resolve outweighed fear and common sense. Tears filled my eyes as I struggled to maintain my gaze on the traffic around me. I wiped my eyes with my shirt sleeve and sat upright in the seat peering through the steering wheel; wavering between remaining inconspicuous or running him over. When we reached her apartment, I caught him glimpse in his rearview mirror and he was startled to see me following him. I immediately returned home as he pursued me. The hurt in my heart for my mom and brother was so great that it took my breath. I clutched my chest from the pain, fearing a heart attack.

I wondered if a healthy 15-year-old girl could have a heart attack? He dropped to his knees, looking up at me with tears of shame and guilt falling from his eyes and begging me to keep his secret from Mom. I cursed him, using words I'd never uttered, and sobbed as a heartbreaking sorrow crushed me because he betrayed me again.

I stood above him, with more power than I knew what to do with and hatred collided with grief. The hatred was greater than I have ever felt. My animal instinct was to grab any heavy object and beat him about the head, but he was still my father. So I reached for a large plant and threw it as hard as I could into the backyard fence, shattering it to pieces, just as my heart had shattered to pieces.

This is but one of many instances that occurred during my childhood, so when I was 16 years old, Mom finally gathered the courage to breach the agreement they made more than a decade earlier. I was proud of her even though I did not yet understand the fullness of the mysterious memory of the Blue Light Motel and the reasons we remained in captivity.

Oftentimes, when a person is wrongfully imprisoned, they are hurled into a rocky crossroad; forced to make decisions they wouldn't normally make. We all lived in survival mode for many years trying to get through the day with no long-term or medium-term plans. Mom married at 16 and gave birth to me 18 months later and my brother three years later. She didn't graduate from high school and never had a job. Her vulnerability and Dad's verbal abuse and aberrant behavior subjugated her to the mighty power he wielded. She understood that escape required a plan and education offered a gateway to enter the work force, preparing a path to our freedom.

No one can fully understand what the impact of years of mental and physical abuse can do to a person's soul unless they've experienced it. Dad had already kidnapped us once and the terms of their agreement were etched in Mom's experience. He was the real deal and years later I understood why she stayed.

I was so grateful when she had readied herself to free us from the bondage after years of arguing, crying, lying, and unsolicited beatings. I was thankful he was going to be out of the house; I didn't want him out of my life, just out of the house because he was still my dad. I didn't want to witness the cheating; didn't want to hear the lies; didn't want to fight; didn't want to cry anymore. I thought if he were out of the house, we could all find peace and there would be no more yelling and fighting. But moving a few blocks away did not take away the demons my dad lived with, nor did his absence remove my constant companions of rebellion, shame, sadness, and loneliness. Dad left, but they didn't. My companions set up residence and I didn't know how to evict them.

Soon thereafter, I began ruminating about the comfort alcohol brought a few years prior. I was 16 years old and too young to buy alcohol, so a friend and I pulled our money together, drove to a local liquor store, parked out of view from the door, and waited for an unsuspecting stupid man to amble by. I viewed most men with disgust and disdain. They were weak and pathetic because with just a little flirting you could get them to do anything. Since I was a young girl, I studied my dad and witnessed how he manipulated situations so that he could escape the family to have sex with his girlfriends. He taught me the power of sex in a relationship. We've got it and they want it. How bad they want it is where the dance begins. Later, as I grew weary of the dance, I stole the booze and hid it in a cabinet in the garage, not too far from where I took that first drink three years earlier.

Dad had been out of the house for about six months and visited often, sometimes the visit was pleasant, and others were wrought with fighting, screaming, door slamming, and tears. Dad was a skilled craftsman and often contracted handyman jobs for extra income. Two weeks after my 17th birthday, he was on his way to a side job and stopped by to pick me up. As a new legal driver, I jumped at any opportunity to drive, but I changed my mind and chose to stay home because something didn't feel quite right.

As I sat in the recliner, I heard the front door shut immediately followed by a light tap on the kitchen window. I turned my head in his direction and we smiled at each other, but the expression of his eyes changed momentarily, and the words that followed were contrite and solemn as he said, "Goodbye, I love you." In an instant, I knew he was going to kill himself. I knew he regretted all that he had done, all that was said, all that I witnessed, so these words did not come as a surprise, nor did the feeling behind them. Many times, when he drank, he'd cry and ramble on, sometimes threatening suicide, about things he had done to my mother, brother, and me. I wasn't filled with panic or a desire to embrace him and plead for his change of heart. Instead, I said, "I love you," and watched him walk out of my life forever, just as I'd hoped for many years. Hours later, the sheriff's deputy knocked on the door and reported that Dad had been in a fatal accident. I couldn't process the word 'fatal' and wanted to go to the hospital, but he was not in the emergency room surrounded by a medical team attempting to revive him, instead he lay on a cold stainless-steel table in the morgue. I felt immense sadness and disgust for him. How can I love this man and hate him? And now I've participated in his demise. What's wrong with me? How am I going to live with myself?

I had no one to yell at and no one to blame; he just left. A gush of unrecognizable feelings encircled me. Since I had no comprehension of how to corral them, I frantically latched on to the only anchor within reach – anger. The irony to this story is Dad had a loving, caring, and committed side. Oftentimes, I thought I was living with two different people because even in the midst of the anguish and confusion, I never questioned his love for me, nor could I forget the few fun memories. Undoubtedly, this is why I vacillated between love and hate. I can only imagine the demons he faced and the companions he carried to his death.

I drank and ran the streets with friends trying to forget about the abuse and trying to forget about Dad. Alcohol wasn't strong enough some of the time, so I started smoking marijuana. Booze and weed were the perfect combination to numb my mind and stunt the growth of my soul. Good and bad choices made during this time set the course for my future, like a captain setting the course of a ship navigating troubled waters. One wrong decision and the ship could come aground or hit an obstacle, sinking the ship.

I didn't know what a good choice was because I had drifted so far from God that choices no longer meant good or bad. I merely stumbled recklessly along a path I chose years earlier. As I journeyed down the trail with shame, rebellion, sadness, and loneliness, I invited my new companion along and her name was anger.

CHAPTER FOUR

The Whisper

I started noticing boys about this time. The combination of alcohol, drugs, boys, and a troubled young girl is akin to playing a game of Russian roulette. Put one bullet in the cylinder, spin it a few times and slowly place the barrel against your temple. You don't want to pull the trigger, but you have to because that's how the game is played. So, you gently, slowly, squeeze the trigger and the gun doesn't fire this time. But eventually it will, and someone will die.

I am a 17-year-old confused and unhappy girl. While out late one night, I came across a boy I had a crush on in high school. I never had a boyfriend and didn't know what to expect. I was drunk and so was he. I had no self-worth and just wanted him to like me. But to me, "just like me" meant I had to do what he said because that's how I survived for years. Unfortunately, "do what he said" meant rape. My first sexual experience was rape by a boy I had a crush on in high school.

Of course, this makes perfect sense because a girl like me couldn't say no. I didn't have the wherewithal to make a proper choice. I wanted to scream out but the words were confined in my mouth. I stayed quiet and whispered "no" so that only my ears could hear. Yelling "no" to him couldn't happen because pleasing and wanting love, co-mingled with feelings of no self-worth, were intertwined into something similar to slippery silk fabric.

The silkworm weaves beautiful silk to form its cocoon. My thoughts about myself were woven by my father into a creation of the cocoon he formed for me. A cocoon is made to protect the creature inside from a harsh environment. My cocoon was woven by a broken man and was frayed and weak. My cocoon couldn't hold and protect me, and when it was time for me to emerge, I was not fully developed and didn't have the ability to withstand the life before me. Therefore, when it came time to cry out "NO!", I didn't say anything at all. But, the little girl dancing on the wooden pew whispered "no" in my ear. She was with me.

Immediately after and in order to protect myself, I started taking birth control pills and stayed on them for the next 21 years. I didn't know what kind of mother I would be and I surely didn't trust men. I was promiscuous because I didn't care about myself. I didn't want to have a child because if Dad could do and say hurtful things to me, so could my husband. I couldn't separate Dad from the men in my life as he and they were the same; dishonest and untrustworthy. I spent the next several years darting from one relationship to the next. I married twice but was never satisfied. I found fault with these men and left them. I found fault with most all of them and left.

As the years went by, the little girl dancing on the wooden pew kept wooing me from time-to-time. On those occasions when I'd get excessively drunk in my attempt to drown the sadness from my soul, she'd whisper, trying to bring me home where I belonged. But I knew I couldn't go home after all I had done. The booze, men, and lies. . .so, I pushed her out of my mind. She could never be part of my life because I was bad and dirty. I'd have a few drinks and laugh with friends – but when it came time to go home, sadness and loneliness filled the hollow space within me.

The little girl dancing on the wooden pew was calling me to join her, but I turned my back and frantically ran in the opposite direction. How could God love me when I'd had sex out of wedlock more times than I could count? How could God love me when I drank and cursed and talked bad about people? It's not possible; so, I'll have another drink and numb my mind, numb my soul, and forget about it.

CHAPTER FIVE

The Appointment

I continued to hide from God as the years went by and men walked in and out of my life. I believed if I didn't talk to God then He couldn't see me and He wouldn't know I existed. If I stayed away from Him and hid in the shadows, then He couldn't see all the bad things I was doing to myself. But one day, Satan – who I had been living for – finally got me just where he wanted. I picked up the gun, put one bullet in the cylinder, spun it a few times, and pulled the trigger. This time the gun went off and someone died.

Satan is a thief, a liar, and a murderer. He was my father at that time, and like any good father, he wanted me to be better than he was. All parents want their children to have a better life than they had and Satan is no exception. I became pregnant and on June 15, 1998, I aborted my child. Satan was so proud of me. Not only did I commit murder, but I murdered my own. I was at the top of my class; valedictorian. He had me in the palm of his hand and he started to wrap his fingers around me and squeeze. Murdering my child wasn't enough for Satan; he wanted me to hate myself and live in shame for the rest of my life and ultimately follow him to Hell.

My loathsome journey to murder was prophetic. I followed the road map I designed for myself through the thousands of bad choices I made, which ultimately led to death's doorstep. I always thought it would be my own death, but it wasn't. I thought of death often and was comforted thinking I would go to sleep and the pain would be over. Many times, I had planned my own death and even helped it along with pills and alcohol, but I always escaped. The little girl dancing on the wooden pew whispered in my ear and told me it would destroy Mom. So, I sucked it up and plowed through another day, another week, another month, another year, another decade.

When I stood at the edge of my world, and looked to the right at the father of my child standing next to me, I asked, "Why him?" He couldn't have been more wrong for me and that is exactly why he was next to me. I panicked when I found I was pregnant. I had never been pregnant and now I'm with Mr. Wrong.

I was 38 years old and fully understood the level of commitment needed to raise a healthy child. He didn't have it and I didn't want to do it with him. The weeks started adding up to months and my internal conversation took over. Honestly, from the moment I read the result of the home pregnancy test I couldn't envision me raising my child with him. I never thought of him as the father because he was not the type of father I wanted for my child. I needed to have enough conversations with myself to justify getting him out of my life. I told myself he would end up in prison. . .and he did. I told myself I didn't want to take my child to prison on visiting day. I told myself I didn't want to share custody with a drug dealer. I told myself I didn't want my child to pay for my mistake. I told myself a lot of things until I finally told myself to pull the trigger.

Mom, who has always been my biggest supporter, left for vacation out of state for a few weeks. Before she left, we talked, and she was willing to babysit and help any way she could. But when Mom left and I didn't have her to talk to every day, I talked to myself. If I was going to do this, it had to be now. Mom was away and I didn't have to explain my decision or look her in the eyes, and I surely couldn't ask her to participate in murdering her grandchild.

It was my choice and I did not want her to be a witness. I've made my bed, now I must lie in it.

I started telling myself that abortion is okay. People do it all the time and it's even covered by insurance. The secular world has convinced most people that abortion is perfectly acceptable for eliminating unwanted pregnancies. *Roe vs. Wade* was decided by the Supreme Court on January 7, 1973, with a 7-to-2 majority vote by highly educated and intelligent people. If the government says it's okay, then it must be. I admit for many years I thought abortion was my choice and I alone had the right to make the decision about my body. I also thought my baby didn't do anything wrong and what chance would my baby have in this mess I created. I convinced myself it was the right thing to do. I convinced myself I was doing my baby a favor. I became the serpent. I deceived myself.

Whenever I saw pro-life fanatics on the side of the road with their signs and gory pictures, I would roll down the window and yell at them saying things like, "It's none of your business" or "You don't know what you're talking about," and some other choice profane words and gestures. This is not the way I normally behave, but I was angry and I wanted them to know they were wrong. I became enraged when I saw men holding signs with pictures of a bloodied fetus and my thoughts were, really, what do they know about it? They can't give birth. They're the ones who put us in this position anyway. They need to stay out of it.

I vehemently embraced this attitude and was proud of my opinion. When family members or friends talked about abortion, I always had a strong viewpoint and most everyone agreed. But one day, I had an abortion and I changed.

I flung the door open to deceit when I made the fateful decision to murder my child. I frantically switched to survival mode and began to thoughtfully plot the devious details of the burial of my shameful secret. A detective recognizes a paper trail is a direct line to apprehending a criminal, and as a murderer, this placed me on the most wanted list. I had to act quickly and methodically to evade detection. I paid in cash to avoid a charge on my insurance and to hide the murder from the human resources department at work. I further covered my tracks and lied to my baby's father, friends, and co-workers saying I had a miscarriage. A common behavior of a murderer is to keep a trophy of their criminal act so they can reminisce. During the first few months of my pregnancy, a co-worker gave me a cream-colored onesie baby outfit covered in tiny yellow and black bumble bees with an embroidered patch of Winnie the Pooh dipping his paw into a pot of "hunny". My trophy was the baby outfit which I kept as a sacred memento. I placed the baby outfit in a box, placed a lid on the top, taped the lid on all four sides, and slid the box on the shelf in the back of a dark dank closet where it remained for years. I should have thrown it away, but I couldn't. I knew that someday the little girl dancing on the wooden pew would call me home. Together, we would take the box off the shelf, gently place it on the table, un-tape the lid, and lovingly, reverently, hold the only thing I have in the physical realm of my child.

I looked in the phonebook and found a phone number of a local abortion clinic. Two days later, I walked past protesters in the parking lot waving those same gory signs with pictures of a bloodied unborn fetus. People behind them yelling "murderer; baby killer" as my head hung and my hair falling to cover my face, the face of shame as I walked quickly toward the front door. The receptionist greeted me in the same way I am greeted at the dentist office or a fast food restaurant, "Hi, can I help you?" But I'm not getting my teeth cleaned or ordering a hamburger and fries. Today I am murdering my child, but the greeting is the same.

I quickly find a seat in the reception area and slowly lift my head halfway and gaze around the room. I see 20-30 women; ages 18–40; every race and socio-economic background. Outside these walls we have little in common, yet this decision unites us. This choice solidifies our eternal fate and we are no longer women of varying age and background, we are killers; killers of our children, our future, and our relationship with God. I wait and I think. I hear my name in the distance. I want to get it over with, yet I feel like I'm walking in quicksand as I move toward the door. The nurse's assistant greets me with a smile and motions me toward a small room. She asked me to read some material about abortion. I have no idea what I am reading because what my eyes are seeing and what my mind is thinking are not meshing. The gears in my brain are stuck on one thing: Will God forgive me? The tears are flowing so quickly and strong that the few tissues I had were soaked and fraying. I'm wiping my face with my shirt sleeve and the sobs are coming from somewhere inside I can't quite identify; maybe my stomach, the top of my head, all the way from my feet, but most likely from my soul. The nurse's assistant kindly asks if I want to talk to someone. All I can say between continuous uncontrollable sobs and gulping for air is, "No, I have to do this." She sweetly asks again and I give her the same response. I'm in it too deep. If I were to change my mind, how do I live knowing I came this close? How do I look at my child knowing I wanted to kill you?

She gently tells me what to expect from my body, that I would experience cramping for a few days similar to heavy menstrual cramps, and spotting that could last up to six weeks. She told me I needed to take antibiotics to ward off any potential infection. She also said I may have a wide range of feelings after the abortion. She told me most women ultimately feel relief and some women feel anger, regret, guilt, or sadness. . .for a little while.

But what is most disturbing to me, and the greatest lie of all, is no one told me of the shame I was to live with. No one told me about the depression and the cloud of sadness I would carry for years. No one told me that when asked if I wanted to hold my baby niece or nephew I would panic, my heart beating quick and fast, and I would have trouble catching my breath. No one told me that each year on the anniversary date I would cry and feel such deep sorrow. No one told me that I would avoid all children because I felt I no longer deserved to be a mother. No one told me that I would learn to hate myself for what I had done. No one told me that it would affect my relationship with my future husband in such a crushing and sad way. No one told me that I could ever fully raise my head again. No one told me that it would damage my life forever. No one told me that it was a SIN!

The nurse asked me to put on a white hospital gown and wait for a few minutes while the doctor prepared for the procedure. I laid on the gurney and they wheeled me down a hallway and through a side door. I could see my gown gently moving up and down on my chest. As they rolled me into the room, shock overcame me as there were three or four women on gurneys; knees drawn, legs separated, feet in stirrups, with a surgical team surrounding each woman; again, being united in a most revolting way.

But something extraordinary happened to me that day. I didn't want God to know what I was doing. I didn't want Him to see me. Surprisingly, the crushing guilt and shame I felt attacking my six senses are exactly what drew me to Him.

I could *HEAR* the doctor gently speaking to me and preparing me for the abortion while the nurses were talking quietly trying to soothe me. I could *SMELL* the chemicals and the gas from the mask as it was about to be placed over my face. I could *SEE* my legs separated with my feet in the stirrups. I could *TASTE* the saliva in my mouth as I gasped and sucked in the air through my salty tears. I could *FEEL* my gown clenched between my fingers as I squeezed and squeezed the fabric, wishing it were someone's hand to hold. But whose would it be? Who could I tell? I didn't want anyone to know. Who would ever understand? My sixth sense of *IMAGINATION* is the most profound and disturbing for me to accept. I imagined my life, carrying the weight of all my companions: rebellion, shame, sadness, loneliness, and anger, and the exhaustion I would feel as I ran and hid from God for the rest of my life.

Yet, amidst the abundant emotions, the waterfall of tears falling from my eyes, and as they placed the mask over my face, I cried out to God begging for forgiveness. I was so ashamed that I hoped God was looking the other way at that moment. I didn't want God to know what I was doing. I deserved to be left alone – I didn't deserve sympathy or comfort, but I did beg for forgiveness. Even though I didn't want Him to see me in this way, He was the first and only one I cried out to. I wanted to hide from Him; hoping He didn't know what I was doing, yet I called His name. As much as I didn't want Him to know, I wanted Him to know. He's the only one who could give me the truth. I knew what I was doing was a sin, but I hoped He would understand and forgive me someday. Why did I call out His name?

I was alone, frightened, ashamed, and doubting my decision. Before I was conceived, a seed had been planted in my soul by God and later cultivated by my Sunday School teachers. The seed lay dormant for many years, but the little girl dancing on the wooden pew was bringing it to life. Even though I was not saved, nor was I walking with God, the little girl dancing on the wooden pew knew

He was the only one who could save me from this grave sin, and that's why I called on Him. The Bible tells me that, "For whosoever shall call upon the name of the Lord shall be saved." (Romans 10:13 KJV). I didn't know it at the time, but something implanted in me many years ago was longing to emerge.

CHAPTER SIX

Living with It

I did not allow myself to mourn after the abortion. I wholeheartedly believed I forfeited my right to mourn; thus, earning a lifetime pass down a well-worn path of shame, guilt, and pain. My secret took a commanding position within me, and when I needed and wanted to, I couldn't cry in front of family, friends, or co-workers. There was no posting in the obituaries announcing the death of my child. There was no funeral ceremony where loving words were shared and tears shed to honor my child. There was nothing. There was a death and a loss of what could have been, but I couldn't tell anyone about it. I didn't bury my child, but I buried my secret. Again, I am the serpent. I am the liar.

As time went by, and in casual conversation, people asked if I had children. Instantly, fear overtook me and my eyes cast down as a feeble attempt to conceal the shameful secret. Similar to the rape years earlier, my mouth formed the word "no" as my hushed voice fought to hold the word or let it go in a grief-stricken whisper. All the while, my heart was cracking under the pressure with my face of stone disguising my pain.

I flung my arrogant cheerleader attitude about abortion rights far from me and began the backbreaking process of building a wall. Every word of denial and whispered lie was one stone placed on another until I was a cowering, scarred, and broken shell. Stone walls were originally built in Mesopotamia thousands of years ago for defense, privacy, and protection of its inhabitants. I built a wall for the same basic reason, but also to hide my secret from onlookers and God. As I constructed the wall, my soul slowly deteriorated by continuously denying my child ever existed. It didn't happen all at once but took several years.

I soon discovered that shame and guilt had slowly smothered my love and compassion. Years earlier, my fire was ignited by childhood rebellion which provided a conduit for thousands of bad choices. Living in California, we have yearly wildfires that take many souls, destroy property, and obliterate thousands of acres of beautiful lush forest. At this time, my fire was only 5% contained and I needed retardant to extinguish the blaze and minimize destruction. I dowsed the wildfire with shame, guilt, drugs, and alcohol and all that remained was a smoldering pile of ashes waiting to reignite. I refused to allow myself to think of God as there was no room for Him because the shame and guilt occupied the hole in my heart. After a few years, there came a day when I couldn't live with myself anymore. I was growing weaker in my soul and I desired healing more than I desired hiding.

I thought if I made it impossible for me to get pregnant, then my price was paid and I might get some relief. I made an appointment and met with a doctor and begged him to sterilize me. This was the only time I had ever been pregnant and look what I had done. I didn't deserve to have a child in my life and I didn't deserve to be a mother.

The doctor was reluctant and tried to talk me out of it. We argued for some time, but after a lot of convincing, I finally talked him into it. I was cut and my female organs cauterized so that I could never bear a child. I was judge, jury, and prosecutor, and I decided that the death of motherhood was my sentence.

I was devastated when I realized the shame still lived in me, even after disfiguring my own body and taking away any chance of motherhood. I'd done all I could do and the shame is still there. So instead, I would meet with friends, have some drinks, laugh and try to forget about it, but I couldn't. The little girl dancing on the wooden pew was waiting for me to come back, but the shame kept me away.

CHAPTER SEVEN

The Race

A ll the while I was drinking and running from my past, the little girl dancing on the wooden pew kept whispering in my ear. I ran a 10-mile disgraceful race that took 40 years to complete and I had grown weary as I crossed the finish line of my journey.

I remember the route as though it were yesterday. Breezing past the first mile marker in my new running shoes and matching outfit as I cast my eyes upon, "You shall have no other gods before me." (Exodus 20:3 NKJV). Immediately, this caught my attention and as I set my pace, thoughts started creeping in. God couldn't mean how I obsessed on my feelings, or the hours spent planning gatherings and exotic vacations with alcohol at the top of the list.

At mile marker 2, I was still moving at a fast-paced click and as I passed, I glanced at a sign that read, "You shall not make for yourself a carved image – any likeness of *anything* that *is* in heaven or above, or that *is* in the earth beneath, or that *is* in the water under the earth." (Exodus 20:4 NKJV). This didn't apply to me. Everyone dreams of a shiny new red sports car, a beautiful home, and surrounding themselves with nice things. Nothing wrong with that. I think about the rest of the scripture from Sunday School and it says, "you shall not bow down to them nor serve them. For I, the LORD your God, *am* a jealous God, visiting the iniquity of the fathers upon the children of the third and fourth *generations* of those who hate Me, but showing mercy to thousands, to those who love Me and keep My commandments." (Exodus 20:5-6 NKJV). As I put one foot in front of the other, I am frightened because I know how I act when I'm jealous, which always stems from a place of hurt. Am I hurting God when I reject Him and live for myself? I don't want to hurt Him, but my sinful journey has been going on too long and He wouldn't want me anyway.

At this point of the race, I'm approaching mile marker 3 and as I get closer, I focus on the banner which reads, "You shall not take the name of the LORD your God in vain, for the LORD will not hold *him* guiltless who takes His name in vain." (Exodus 20:7 NKJV). I ponder this as I pass. I have taken the Lord's name in vain thousands of times and nothing happened to me. A bolt of lightning didn't fall from the sky and blow me to pieces. Yet, I'm a fool because I don't recognize that I'm in the most pain ever because I have rejected and disrespected Jesus for years. It's not always something as instantaneous and final as a bolt of lightning. That would be easier than living through this godless life I created. So, I keep running but I notice I'm breathing deeper trying to get more blood to my heart. The same heart that is emotionally hollow and desperately needs the blood of Jesus for forgiveness of my sins. Keep running Rhonda!

My thighs are burning, but I know I'm almost halfway to the finish line, so I press on. Mile marker 4 reads, "Remember the Sabbath day, to keep it holy. Six days you shall labor and do all your work, but the seventh day *is* the Sabbath of the LORD your God. *In it* you shall do no work: you, nor your son, nor your daughter, nor your male servant, nor your female servant, nor your cattle, nor your stranger who *is* within your gates. For *in* six days the LORD made the heavens and the earth, the sea, and all that *is* in them, and rested the seventh day. Therefore, the LORD blessed the Sabbath day and hallowed it." (Exodus 20:8-11 NKJV). I live in America and, if you are a Baby Boomer, resting means you are lazy. Working 40+ hours a week, maintaining a neat household, preparing meals, and laundry leaves a day for me to have a good time because I deserve it after the week I've had. Sunday church and rest never occurred to me because my sabbath consisted of many cocktails, marijuana, backyard barbeques, and drunken chatter with friends. As I'm breathing deeper and feeling a bit light-headed, a fleeting memory passes of a feeble attempt to return to church approximately 25 years ago. I recall walking into the sanctuary at Christian Life Center and feeling such immense conviction that the tears poured from my eyes as I franticly ran out before the sermon began. The little girl dancing on the wooden pew was trying to get my attention.

Mile marker 5 says, "Honor your father and your mother, that your days may be long upon the land which the LORD your God is giving you." (Exodus 20:12 NKJV). It's easy to honor my mother, but there is no way I'm going to honor my father. I take full responsibility for the choices I made but my father did have an impact on my development, which fueled the decisions I made and where I am today running this exhausting race.

My muscles are getting weak and I'm feeling disoriented from mild dehydration. I grab a bottle of cool water, take a few sips, and pour the rest over my head. As the water rolls down my face, I pass mile marker 6 and I read, "You shall not murder." (Exodus 20:13 NKJV). I would never do anything like that. I had an abortion because I was doing my child a favor. An abortion is not murder because it's legal and our government pays for it!

I see mile marker 7 in the distance, but I'm still ruminating on the abortion. My questioning mind starts moving slow like a steam locomotive, chugging along the tracks with question after question, building up speed. A steam engine needs combustible material to produce steam. The steam moves through reciprocating pistons which are connected to the wheels and away we go. Doubt is the steam that moves through the pistons in my mind which are connected to my actions. So, I ask, "Could that have been murder?" When I entered the abortion clinic, I had a fetus with a beating heart inside my womb and a few hours later the fetus was dead. A medical professional used a vacuum-type instrument and sucked my baby out of my womb in pieces, placed the pieces of my baby in a red plastic bag, and laid my baby's remains on a shelf ready for disposal or possibly harvested my baby's organs and sold for profit. How would I know? I ran to my car so quickly to avoid judgmental onlookers and pro-life ranters. Yet, I gave my child to Satan on a silver platter and allowed strangers to destroy the evidence in an incinerator under the guise of 'medical waste.' What happens when someone is put in an incinerator? Well, the Nazi's would know all about that. It's the best most efficient way to eliminate unwanted people and remove all evidence of a crime. The process is completed in stages; 1) dehumanize the individual; 2) convince your community to agree to your interpretation; and 3) eliminate the problem.

Oh my gosh, how did I fall for the greatest lie of all? I am such an idiot! I know I had a lot of help from Satan and I'm sure he was pleased because he deceived another. His lie was twofold: murder of the future, and destruction of the mother's relationship with God if she doesn't repent. Satan is separated from God, and will do anything to keep me in the same prison. He's also the master of deception and deceived a society that has either rejected God or chooses to cherry pick their way through the Bible. I hadn't fully rejected God, but I certainly was running from Him, trying to hide in the shadows hoping He was busy with someone else's messed up life, thinking I could slip past Him. I'm such a loser!

I'm so tired at this point of the race and am breathing hard, as I recall how I lied to myself so that I could get through it only to realize the end was just the beginning. My thoughts are gathering momentum and moving down the track at a high rate of speed. Then I think about the pro-choice mantra I use to rant, "Reproductive Rights are Human Rights." Isn't a baby a human? Didn't Sunday School classes discuss King David saying something about knitting you in your mother's womb? For so long, I fooled myself into believing that I had the right to make the decision over my body. Who was looking out for my baby? It should have been me and I failed horribly.

We have made abortion too easy. It's more difficult to open a bank account than to murder your child. The abortion clinic didn't have a checklist to meet a criterion. I didn't even have to come up with a plausible lie for the paperwork because there wasn't any. Yet, to end my child's life and destroy my relationship with Jesus, I enter an abortion clinic and am out within hours. How did we get to this place in a country founded on Christianity, where the Bible is very specific about Jesus' thoughtful plan for each of us? How did I drift so far away? I'm on this tangent and people are passing me left and right because I'm not concentrating on my breathing and I'm falling behind. These thoughts are rifling through my mind and I can't stop thinking about this scripture.

I am stumbling along and breathing heavy when I come upon the next banner, "You shall not commit adultery." (Exodus 20:14 NKJV). Well yes, but I was a different person and I felt very shameful about this. Remember, it takes two! Besides, I had this ingenious idea that if I dated married men, they wouldn't get too serious and want to move in with me. I could keep them under control by using the tools my father taught.

I'm coming to the end of the race and as I turn near mile marker 8, my foot lands in small pothole and I twist my ankle. I look up and see, "You shall not steal." (Exodus 20:15 NKJV). I don't steal, although I have stolen my health, my memory, relationships, and opportunities by my lifestyle. I must keep going because I'm nearing the end. How am I going to make it with this injury? Runners know how to keep going through the pain. I push the pain out of my mind and will deal with it later, just like everything else in my life.

A young girl is waving a sign at mile marker 9 and it says, "You shall not bear false witness against your neighbor." (Exodus 20:16 NKJV). What does that mean? All I can think of is my swollen, aching ankle, yet I remember telling little white lies from time-to-time just to keep the peace. That's what alcoholics do in order to minimize situations so that we can deal with them. Also, for years, as the self-assigned family secret-bearer, I lied to my mother to protect her and my brother.

I turn the corner and the finish line is ahead, but I'm hobbling, my legs are so heavy, my lungs are aching and I don't think I've ever been this tired. One more mile to go and it's mile marker 10 which says, "You shall not covet your neighbor's house; you shall not covet your neighbor's wife, nor his male servant, nor his female servant, nor his ox, nor his donkey, nor anything that *is* your neighbor's." (Exodus 20:17 NKJV). I've never been an envious person. I'm happy with what I have and I have everything I need. When I see someone is happy, I am happy for them. However, when I see someone filled with joy, I am not joyful for them because I don't know what joy feels like. Why don't I feel that way? Happiness can come and go, but joy is something deep within. Joy comes from somewhere else. What makes them so darned joyful? I need to get away from them.

As I stagger and stumble across the finish line, I fall to the ground and realize I have broken every Commandment from God. I ran my disgraceful race alone and was proud of it, until I reached the finish line and realized that if I had asked for help and submitted to Jesus along the way, I wouldn't be this broken. These laws are not like the laws that our Congress passes or the Supreme Court upholds. These laws were written by the God that spoke us into existence thousands of years ago. "And when He had made an end of speaking with him on Mount Sinai, He gave Moses two tablets of the Testimony, tablets of stone, written with the finger of God." (Exodus 31:18 NKJV).

As I look back now, I see God was intervening in my life and preparing me for His work. The prophet Jeremiah conveyed, "For I know the plans I have for you,' declares the LORD, 'plans to prosper you and not to harm you, plans to give you hope and a future.'" (Jeremiah 29:11 NIV). This is a beautiful promise in the Bible, but at that time, this scripture was written for someone else. These prophetic words written over 2,500 years ago could not be meant for someone like me.

CHAPTER EIGHT

Rehab

T welve years after the abortion, I found myself in a situation where even I knew God had His hand all over it. I had a personnel issue with a co-worker and we mutually agreed to seek counseling as a remedy to our conflict. By this time, I am married to my third husband, Jimmie. Little did I know, but God had a wonderful plan for the two of us. I met alone with a counselor at employee options and after a few minutes talking with her, she asked me if I drank. I was surprised by the question because this had nothing to do with why I was there. I told her I did. . .not every day, but I could drink a bottle of champagne by myself on a Saturday afternoon (more like two if I were honest) and a few visits to the bar throughout the week. She handed me a questionnaire to take home, complete it, and return in a day. As I reached for the papers, I noticed the title of the questionnaire was, "Are You an Alcoholic?" Immediately, my hands shook as I clutched the papers in my hands, and the tears started to flow down my cheeks. The emotions I thought I had so cleverly buried began to spill over and there was no containing them.

I completed the questionnaire and returned in a day. As I handed her the papers, she took them from me and sat back in her chair not uttering a word. She stared at me for a few more moments and I became uncomfortable and squirmed in my chair. I asked her what was wrong and she said, "I have been doing this type of counseling for 27 years and no one, I mean no one, has ever completed the questionnaire." My body shook as I squeezed my eyes together to hold back the tears. I couldn't hide anymore. She could see me. I was exposed.

I told her I filled out the papers with the help of my mom and step-dad, and I also wrote examples on the back of the questionnaire. She was speechless and stared at me for a moment longer. I didn't know what to say and was searching for words to fill in the empty space. After a moment, she gently placed the papers on her desk, turned and looked me in the eyes. She took a deep breath and said, "Will you go to a 28-day residential rehab facility?" I took a deep exhausted breath and said, "Yes." God was reaching out to me and I could feel His presence. This was a God-thing and I knew it. I was beginning my journey – coming out of the darkness and moving toward the light. I left on November 19, 2010, and returned home before Christmas and have never looked back. I went to a couple of Alcoholics Anonymous meetings, but I just couldn't connect. I knew I was on the right path, but something was missing I couldn't identify.

CHAPTER NINE

Salvation

A bout one year later, Mom was diagnosed with an incurable life-threatening disease. She was raised on church pews and taught to love and fear the Lord. Since she walked away from God decades earlier, she had a deep-seated belief that her sins separated her from God and she feared where backsliding had taken her. Mom thoroughly understood she had come face-to-face with hell, and the realization of death without salvation terrified her. Backsliding is an Old Testament term used to describe those who have been near to God but have allowed sin to take them away from Him. Backsliding can be caused by many things; however, whatever the sins might be that led her away from God, she knew that they must be dealt with honestly and brought before Him in repentance. God loves us and wants us to be close to Him. Even when we sin against Him, He promises to forgive. "I will heal their backsliding, I will love them freely: for mine anger is turned away from him." (Hosea 14:4 KJV).

The seed planted in her decades ago was straining to push through the hard-packed soil as she was being drawn to the Lord. She got on-line and searched for Christian Life Center where she saw a picture of her childhood friend from 50 years ago. Mom decided to go to church the following Sunday, but Satan persistently pursued her by attacking her mind and she stayed away. A few days later, on an early Monday morning, she was doing her weekly grocery shopping. She strolled through the market placing items in her basket and as she neared the checkout line, she recognized a woman. The woman caught her attention because she was surrounded by light. Not a fluorescent light hanging from the ceiling highlighting a holiday display of cookies and chocolates, but a warm and glowing sunlight that drew her near. The woman was Joy Haney whom Mom had not seen in 50 years!

Mom was astonished and immediately recognized what had happened in the spirit realm. Joy was equally surprised and told Mom it would be the best birthday gift if she would come to church this Easter Sunday and sit next to her on the pew. Mom was frightened and had been searching for healing. I love my mom very much and thought I would go this one time to support her. I was excited for Mom, but there was no excitement for me and thought of it as any other day. This was all about Mom and her healing.

I met Mom in the parking lot and we walked toward the church. We were greeted by the many friendly greeters at the entrance and then walked toward the door to the sanctuary. I opened the door for Mom, and as I followed her down the aisle, I felt a tug. It sounds crazy, but I felt the squeeze of a hand tenderly clutch my collar and pull me gently but firmly toward the altar. I had no fear even though the hand did not let go. I sat down and the tears started flowing and flowing and flowing as my body trembled. I know now this was the power of God's spirit flowing over me like cool water in a dry desert. I don't remember the pastor's sermon, I just remember crying – an uncontrollable, inconsolable crying. I've experienced crying in this fashion often throughout my life, but these tears spring forth from the little girl dancing on the wooden pew. She is the best part of me and I'm listening to her for the first time.

Something profound happened to me and I felt an earth-shaking shift in my soul. I couldn't wait to return to church, and a week later, I again cried through the entire service. At the altar call, I noticed the lights reflecting off the water and onto the back wall from the baptismal. My eyes were fixated on the baptismal and all I could think was, "Isn't someone going to ask me if I want to be baptized?"

My body was trembling inside and I had a strong desire for healing that had to be filled. I had tunnel vision and could only see what was directly in front of me. At the end of the service, there were many people milling around the sanctuary, chatting and praying, but I could neither see nor feel their presence. All I could hear was a low murmur and sound waves moving around me. I felt I was having an out-of-body experience. My body was there with everyone and I was part of the movement, but my mind and eyes were focused on the baptismal.

Finally, someone tapped me on the shoulder and when I turned toward the voice, I looked and saw Rene Marie. She quietly and sweetly asked if I would like to see the baptismal and I immediately said yes. I spent decades immersed in the filth of my decisions and I desperately needed the cleansing power of a Jesus' name baptism. As I came up out of the water with my head raised with lifted hands, I felt clean for the first time since my days dancing on the wooden pew.

The following Sunday, I received the Holy Ghost. I wanted the Holy Ghost so bad and it was on my mind throughout the week. I needed His promised gift and desperately desired His forgiveness. I admit I was a bit afraid at first because in my naiveté, I thought I may get the Holy Ghost while shopping, or in exercise class, and the paramedics would be called because I was speaking in tongues. Fortunately, it doesn't work like that.

The precursor to my Holy Ghost experience came with a wonderful surprise. I have suffered from insomnia for many years, and the night before I received God's promise, I slept the entire night and woke up refreshed because He came to me in a life-saving dream.

In my dream, I pictured a dirt covered alley with a few potholes. The alley was narrow with enough space for one car to pass and a foot or so on either side. On the left was a wood fence in need of painting and leaning a bit. There were mustard weeds growing from the bottom of the fence with a few soft yellow flowers. On the right was a chain-linked fence about three feet high. Overgrown Mulberry trees from the backyards hung over the fence and shaded the roadway. The alley was empty except for me standing on the east end. But what is most significant is what was at the other end of the alley. As I look toward the west end of the alley, it became narrow, like a tunnel; so narrow, yet so far that I couldn't see the end because there was no end. I felt a presence and a light drawing me near. I don't see God, but I know He's there waiting for me.

I dreamt that God was coming and taking His people home and I kept saying over and over, "Wait for me. Wait for me." I was running toward Him, stumbling and crying, with a sense of panic while reaching my arms to Him. I didn't feel He was leaving me. I felt He was waiting for me because I'm coming.

When I shared my story with my friend Nancy Widhalm, she said this described a scripture in the book of Matthew, "Enter by the narrow gate; for wide *is* the gate and broad *is* the way that leads to destruction, and there are many who go in by it. Because narrow *is* the gate and difficult *is* the way which leads to life, and there are few who find it." (Matthew 7:13-14 NKJV).

I carried my companions of rebellion, shame, sadness, loneliness, and anger for many years and the only gate we could squeeze through was the broad gate that led to destruction. But I knew from my dream and with God's love and forgiveness, I could abandon those companions and enter through the narrow gate that leads to life.

Decades earlier, and in preparation for this time, the Sunday School teachings and my grandparents' prayers began the construction of the foundation for the little girl dancing on the wooden pew. I didn't know it, but my foundation was built on a rock and could withstand any storm. "Therefore whoever hears these sayings of Mine, and does them, I will liken to a wise man who built his house on the rock: and the rain descended, the floods came, and the winds blew and beat on that house; and it did not fall, for it was founded on the rock. But everyone who hears these sayings of Mine, and does not do them, will be like a foolish man who built his house on the sand: and the rain descended, the floods came, and the winds blew and beat on that house; and it fell. And great was its fall." (Matthew 7:24-27 NKJV). There were countless occasions during my tumultuous journey where I didn't feel that I had any foundation at all, but feelings lie, and somehow, I always held on. The holding on was my bedrock foundation that kept me joined to the Father.

In Jerusalem, there is a large limestone which is approximately 45' long, 12' high and 13' deep and weighs approximately 600 tons. This solid stone forms part of the Western Wall and is one of the largest building blocks in the world. As magnificent as this one stone is, it can't compare to God's foundation. Years earlier, I began constructing a sandstone wall to cower behind in a pathetic attempt to hide from the all-knowing, all-seeing God, all the while, unaware that I was building my wall atop God's foundation. When a mason removes a stone wall, they start with breaking up the mortar which holds the stones together. The rains of shame descended, as the flood of anger came, and the winds of guilt blew and beat the mortar, slowly chipping away; one sin at a time. The stones began to move and sway and ultimately crash and shatter at the top of my Heavenly Father's foundation.

The sinful wall I built was destroyed and I'm exposed, yet excited when I awake because I am going to church today. I am going to receive the gift of the Holy Ghost because God is waiting for me. Pastor Nathaniel Haney began his sermon by saying he felt he was going to do something different today. He said he could feel the Lord's presence and he was going to let it flow. The congregation joyfully shouted. He asked people to come to the altar and they quickly approached one-by-one. Sister Joy Haney took me by the hand and led me to the altar. Mom was next to me and Sister Kim Haney stepped over and began to pray for me. They were teaching me how to ask God into my life and how to surrender.

I wanted the Holy Spirit in me, but I still held onto my shame. I was insecure and uncomfortable raising my hands to the Lord. As my sisters in Christ prayed for me, I cried and shed tears from years of sadness and pain. I wanted to let go, but part of me was hanging on because I didn't believe I fully deserved His forgiveness. How could He forgive me? I've done shameful things. As I freely wept and repented for my sins, I asked God to "take it from me." I kept asking Him over and over to "take it from me, take it from me." I felt a change brewing in my body. My arms started to slowly rise and my tongue began to swell on both sides. My tongue felt so big that it took up all the space in my mouth and back of my throat. I felt as though a hand were gripping the sides of my throat and gently squeezing. When I tried to say, "take it from me," my words were unclear and I was babbling as I felt Him taking my shame. He removed one more sin with every babbled request. My right hand was shaking uncontrollably, my shirt was wet from perspiration, and I could feel sweat rolling down the back of my legs. I was praying so hard and with such remorse for all the sinning I had done that I was getting light headed. I desperately wanted it out of me.

I know the room was full of people, but I neither saw nor heard anyone. My body and mind were in full motion, yet there was no movement around me. My knees weakened and I felt myself buckling and becoming limp. All the energy I took to hold my shame inside so that no one could see was leaving me and my hard-hearted foundation was crumbling. My sinful foundation of rebellion, shame, sadness, loneliness, and anger was being kicked out from under me and I was falling into God's arms. I did exactly what my father preached a lifetime ago. "Then Peter said unto them, 'Repent, and be baptized every one of you in the name of Jesus Christ for the remission of sins, and ye shall receive the gift of the Holy Ghost.'" (Acts 2:38 KJV). The Lord immediately filled me with the gift of the Holy Ghost and I spoke in tongues. I felt His gentle love flowing over and around me. I never experienced anything like this before and thought if this is what salvation feels like, then I'm in!

My precious Jesus had His eye on me for years and never gave up on me even when I rejected Him. He also kept my mom for decades when she rejected Him too. His mercy is unending, overflowing, and for everyone to experience. He performed a miracle in Mom's life and healed her from the life-threatening incurable disease. She is healthy and strong and is a walking testimony to God's healing power. Amen!

CHAPTER TEN

The Box

Salvation is immediate, but acceptance and healing took time for me. The negative self-talk had been whispering to me for years; criticizing and disgracing me for the abortion and all the other sins I committed. I buried my shame and numbed my emotions by drinking and running my disgraceful race from God. As I had done with the trophy, I put all my feelings in a box, placed a lid on the top, taped the lid on all four sides, and slid the box on a shelf in the back of a dark dank closet where it remained for years. I should have thrown it away, but I couldn't. I knew that someday the little girl dancing on the wooden pew, in the black velvet dress with a white lace collar; white tights with ruffles on the bottom, and black patent-leather shoes with shiny silver buckles would call me home. Together, we would take the box off the shelf, place it on the table, un-tape the lid, and dump the contents.

About five months after being born again and receiving the Holy Ghost, my niece Erika Irons gave me the phone number of a counselor at the Pregnancy Resource Center in Lodi, California, (aka Directions Medical Clinic). I must say when God reeled me in, He knew He had to set the hook and get me in the boat quickly.

I met with a thoughtful and compassionate counselor and we completed a 10-week Christian-based post-abortion counseling course. I threw myself into the course and worked tirelessly to learn the ways of God. When I began my journey, people kept telling me that God loves me and He is my healer, my provider, my counselor, and that they love Him too. I couldn't relate to any of this and felt there was something wrong with me. I knew I was where I should be, and I could feel a dramatic change within me, but I didn't feel love for Him because I didn't know Him.

My love affair with the Lord began as a waltz. A waltz is a dance performed by two people who remain close to each other in effortless harmony. The Lord is a gentleman, something I knew nothing about given my past experiences with men. When I read His Word, I felt Him wooing me through His promises in the Bible. Fear reared up in me again because my earthly father lied most of the time and I admit I resisted referring to the Lord as "my father." The word father represented lies, hurt, abuse, and anger; therefore, calling the Lord my father didn't make sense to me because of the contradiction. But the Lord was different from my earthly father because the Bible says, "God *is* not a man, that He should lie, Nor a son of man, that He should repent. Has He said, and will He not do? Or has He spoken, and will He not make it good?" (Numbers 23:19 NKJV). These words gave me permission to speak the word "father" in a loving, kind, and honest way. The way my creator intended it to be spoken by His child. He waited patiently for years on the sidelines, looking in my direction for me to make eye contact with Him.

The post-abortion counseling course taught me about the ways of God. I slowly began to trust Him as He revealed His character to me through His Word in the Bible. I was able to accept His forgiveness because I got to know His nature. I always knew, even as a little girl dancing on the wooden pew, that God forgives, but until I accept His forgiveness, it's not mine. If I hand you a $20 bill, it's not yours until you accept it. I could only accept God's forgiveness by learning who He is.

Also, during the course of study, there was an issue that plagued me and I spoke to my counselor about the dirty and vile feelings I had about myself during and after I was intimate with my husband. I assumed that once I took my traditional marital vows from a minister that my marriage would be new and fresh. My counselor explained that I needed to repent for all the previous relationships I had with men because each time I was intimate with my husband, these men came with me. I immediately repented and the filth of past sexual relations washed away and I was clean. I feel that someone may be struggling with this issue and I encourage you to repent before Jesus and accept His forgiveness. Remember that God's mercy is bigger than our mess.

I wasted years by choosing a sinful life, but when God came to me in a dream, and I finally listened to the little girl dancing on the wooden pew and returned to Him with a repentant heart, it was as if He had been waiting up all night for me. He was sitting on the couch in the living room, in the dark, waiting for me to come through the front door. When I opened the door and came in, I was calling His name. He reached over and turned on the lamp next to the sofa and then and there we saw each other – in the light. As the old gospel song Amazing Grace says, "*I was lost, but now I'm found.*"

CHAPTER ELEVEN

Savannah

A fter completing the course, and with the advice of my counselor, she recommended I pray and ask Jesus to reveal the sex of my child. One evening while in prayer, I asked the question, "Jesus, would you please tell me the sex of my child?" As I lay on my bed, a peaceful spirit filled the room and warm tears began to roll down my cheeks and onto my pillow. I don't know if you have ever had a word from God, but I did not hear His voice. I felt an answer in my spirit is the best way I can describe my experience. My friend Dolores Alaniz shared that when she receives a word from God, she knows it in her "knower." That is what I felt when I asked Jesus to reveal the sex of my child.

Before a child is born, parents spend time thinking of a name and because I accepted God's forgiveness, I was overjoyed at the opportunity to name my child. I journeyed from shame to love all through the power of the Holy Spirit and God's everlasting love for me. When I prayed to Jesus, I knew I could trust Him to be honest and thoughtful because He cannot lie. I could only obtain this from the one who created me. I thought this was the end of the experience, but I had opened the door to something miraculous and had no idea that my daughter Savannah and I were about to embark on our journey of truth and reconciliation.

On January 12, 2014, during a Sunday morning service, Pastor Haney preached a spirit-filled sermon titled, "God's Not Through." I felt a rumbling in my spirit and believed the Lord wanted me to meet my daughter. Feelings of anxiousness, joy, and excitement were building. I don't know what's going to happen next, but I know it's going to be spectacular. I would not have been so bold to think that I deserved this opportunity before understanding the character of God, but knowing Him in an intimate way, I understood that this is what He wanted for me all along.

At the end of the sermon and during the altar call, which thankfully we have at every service, I humbly submitted myself to the Lord and began to earnestly pray. I prayed in anticipation and spoke in tongues with a specific prayer in mind: Lord, I am ready.

The Lord had been preparing me for this moment through the promises in His Word, and in His all-knowing power revealed a detailed vision of my daughter. I can see her in my mind as I write. Savannah is about eight years old. She has tightly curled golden-brown hair with shimmering gold highlights on the ends. Her hair is a bit longer than shoulder length, and the curls gently frame her face. Her hair is a prominent feature that I remember. She is wearing a white cotton empire waist dress with a scoop neckline. There are about six or seven white fabric covered buttons that start at the top of the neckline and end high above the waist. She is not wearing shoes, and I feel she has never worn shoes. An angel, her angel that has been with her all these years, drapes her arm around Savannah as her hand rests gently on her shoulder. Savannah is behind her angel and peeks around to look at me. Her angel is smiling as she looks at Savannah and then at me. No words are spoken, yet Savannah knows who I am. I know I should run and hold her, but we are both bashful with each other because this is our first meeting. I can't move, I only look at her and am thankful she is not angry with me, as this was something that deeply troubled me for years. I sense she wants to know me. She knows we are to be together, but she finds comfort and safety with her angel. It's not our time yet.

I sat on the pew on that regular Sunday morning service with no language to describe the feelings that flowed through me in the spirit as God revealed Savannah to me in such a personal way. Years ago, when I was running my disgraceful race and witnessed joy in others, I turned and ran in the opposite direction. This day I understood and ran toward the joy of the Lord as He has given me something that no man could. . .love. The tears fell from my eyes in a heavy stream. My tears washed the stain of pain from me and cleansed my spirit. I felt clean and refreshed knowing in my knower that Savannah is not angry with me and is eagerly anticipating our time together. This moment of restoration can only be experienced through pursuing a relationship with Jesus Christ.

A few months later, Christian Life Center was planning a Holy Land trip to Israel. I never thought of traveling to Israel, but shortly after my wondrous spiritual introduction to Savannah, I started feeling a tug toward the trip. I spoke to my husband Jimmie and we agreed this would be a life-changing trip I needed to experience and he fully supported me.

On March 22, 2014, I embarked on a 10-day Holy Land Tour to Israel with 96 fellow pilgrims. I knew God had something special planned for me and the trip would be transformative and open another door to my relationship with Savannah. I was naïve and thought the trip would be blissful and spiritual and I would be completely protected. Little did I know when I lowered my armor, Satan would come after me with a vengeance.

We were about three days into our journey and of course I was missing my husband terribly, but my travel companion, Gloria Armenta, was wonderful and so joyful that she prayed me through some of the lonely moments I experienced. She carries a peace with her that can only be known by loving the Lord. I admire her greatly.

On one of our many excursions, we gathered on a boat on the Sea of Galilee. The day was overcast and the seas were calm, unlike the stories of the Bible. Everyone seemed to be enjoying the experience in their own way. We were singing and worshiping God and it was a peaceful and reflective time. As I stood on the back of the boat and looked over the calm water, I heard a voice whispering in my ear. God has never talked to me in an audible voice, but this voice was audible. The voice was Satan's and he was speaking softly, calmly, and in an all-knowing manner; like a father giving loving advice to his daughter. He whispered, "What are you doing here with these people?" "You don't belong here." "You're a phony." "Why don't you just jump into the water right now and sink to the bottom."

I looked over the side of the boat at the water rushing by and glanced around at the other pilgrims. I was instantly flooded with comfortable suicidal thoughts I carried years ago. Heavy feelings of sadness wrapped around me tightly and I wondered if anyone would notice if I slid quietly into the water and sank to the bottom. I did not outwardly react to Satan's taunting. In fact, a month later, I saw a video of the boat trip and I witnessed myself at exactly the time Satan was speaking to me. I gave no indication that he was encouraging me to end it all. I had been here many times in my life when something evil was done or said to me, and I learned to shut down and place the mask of stone over my face. No one was going to see me hurt or frightened.

The familiar feelings of self-doubt, insecurity with my peers, and loneliness reared up and overtook me. Satan carefully stalked me and at just the right time, he knew what to say and how to say it. But he was in for a surprise because this time I had someone on my side I never called on before. All those years of fighting alone and falling deeper into sin with no life preserver were over. I remembered some of the most powerful words I have learned in my Christian walk. "I rebuke you in the name of Jesus Christ of Nazareth!" I immediately took control and threw Satan off the boat. I told him to just jump into the water right now and sink to the bottom. He rocked me because I was not expecting him to travel on the plane with me on my spiritual journey with God. He was supposed to stay in Stockton! I immediately put on my armor because I knew he was looming around waiting to attack. As the Bible states, "Finally, my brethren, be strong in the Lord and in the power of His might. Put on the whole armor of God, that you may be able to stand against the wiles of the devil. For we do not wrestle against flesh and blood, but against principalities, against powers, against the rulers of the darkness of this age, against spiritual *hosts* of wickedness in the heavenly *places*. Therefore take up the whole armor of God, that you may be able to withstand in the evil day, and having done all, to stand. Stand therefore, having girded your waist with truth, having put on the breastplate of righteousness, and having shod your feet with the preparation of the gospel of peace; above all, taking the shield of faith with which you will be able to quench all the fiery darts of the wicked one. And take the helmet of salvation, and the sword of the Spirit, which is the word of God; praying always with all prayer and supplication in the Spirit, being watchful to this end with all perseverance and supplication for all the saints." (Ephesians 6:10-18 NKJV).

A day or so later, we traveled south on Highway 90 passing around the West Bank and Jericho enroute to Jerusalem. On the journey, we stopped for a young shepherd boy on a donkey quickly guiding his flock of sheep across the road, sped by meticulously manicured orchards filled with row upon row of date palm trees, and saw dilapidated wood sheds covered with blue plastic tarps used as housing for nomadic families. We observed camels grazing on green pasture land, barbed wire fences warning of danger, and checkpoints. The realities of a different way of life, in a land that is woven in beauty and danger stirred emotions of excitement and expectation as we anxiously awaited our first gaze upon the most renowned city in the world. As we breached the horizon, and the bus entered Jerusalem, the song "The Holy City" was playing on the intercom and brought tears of joy and peace to many. It was a beautiful moment for us all as we reached the pinnacle of our journey.

Our first stop was the Mount of Olives where Pastor Haney described Jesus' return. "And in that day His feet will stand on the Mount of Olives, Which faces Jerusalem on the east. And the Mount of Olives shall split in two, From east to west, *Making* a very large valley; Half of the mountain shall move toward the north And half of it toward the south." (Zechariah 14:4-5 NKJV). This was one of many moments I stood in awe as I gazed upon the golden dome mounted atop the Temple Mount wondering how someone like me could be in a place like this.

We then descended the hill and strolled through the Jewish Cemetery on our way to the Garden of Gethsemane. The Lord was about to open another door to my healing and I didn't know it. What I did know was Satan was hot on my trail, yet I remained faithful to the Lord awaiting His promised blessing.

The Garden of Gethsemane is the place where Jesus prayed with His disciples the night before He was crucified. Adjacent to the Garden of Gethsemane is the Church of All Nations, a Roman Catholic church open to all Christian denominations. The church enshrines a section of bedrock where Jesus is said to have prayed the night of His arrest. As I entered the church, my eyes were fixed on the nave and the vault which are adorned in mosaics as blue as the Mediterranean Sea. I sat on a small wooden bench at the side of the church, soaking in the mood and moment. I leaned my head back, resting on the wall, and closed my eyes welcoming a conversation, a word, a time with Jesus. As the spirit enveloped me, Jesus in His loving grace spoke to me in my heart and said, "You will get to know your daughter THROUGH ME before you die." How do I describe a word from my Heavenly Father? Not just any word, but one that has the power to remove decades of shame, regret, disappointment, hurt, and sorrow. When I received His promise in my heart, knowing it to be true because He cannot lie, the peace and joy filled me to the brim and weakened my knees as though I had just received a loving embrace to my heart and I could not stand. The tears poured down my cheeks and onto my lap as my hands shook. In the background, I heard people leaving the church and knew I had to walk out, but I did not want to leave, nor did I want this visitation with the Lord to end. I thought the vision of Savannah a few months prior was all there would be and that was more than I ever imagined or deserved. But then the Lord reaches out to me again with a promise of relationship and motherhood.

CHAPTER TWELVE

Back Home

When I returned from Israel, I walked in expectation waiting to receive God's promise. True to His word, at a Sunday morning church service, a young child of three or four walked through the door. The child's shoulder-length hair was identical to that of Savannah's in my spirit vision. The soft curls gently framing her face with golden highlights that sparkled as the light reflected off the curls. My eyes were fixed on the child's hair and I knew in my knower that God was reminding me of His promise. I felt tears welling up; tears of joy that come from my Heavenly Father. I previously shared my vision of Savannah with my mom and when she saw the child, we looked at each other, speechless, as she had the same revelation.

A few months later, at a Ladies Advance conference at Christian Life Center, I earnestly prayed seeking Jesus and He blessed me with another spiritual encounter. Savannah is older and I sense she is not wary of me as she slowly moves toward me opening her arms. Years ago, I buried my gentle motherly nature because those feelings were meant for Savannah and never to be shared with another. But I feel them pushing through, yearning to bare them to the one they were created for. Only Jesus could give me the courage to drop the cold metal shield around my heart because He is love and wants us to share our love with everyone, not hold it tightly because we've been hurt. Savannah would want me to share this part of me with others too. The waters of healing are calm and deep and I don't know what's under the slow-moving current. Jesus, please show me because I'm ready to go deeper. I love you Savannah.

A little time passes and I had been praying and fasting and Savannah spoke to me in my heart. Fasting is an important part of our spiritual walk with God because this is how we humble ourselves before Him by acknowledging His greatness and our limitations. Fasting refreshes the heart and we are better equipped to deal with trials because we are aligned with God and the power of the Holy Spirit. Fasting also puts legs to our prayers and breaks strongholds which entrap us. The book of Isaiah says, "*Is* this not the fast that I have chosen: To loose the bonds of wickedness, To undo the heavy burdens, To let the oppressed go free, And that you break every yoke?" (Isaiah 58:6 NKJV).

I sought God and was open to anything at this moment and Savannah spoke to my heart in a clear voice and said, "Don't be afraid." Oh my! Not only is my daughter alive in the spirit, she is speaking to me, and comforting, advising, and encouraging me to tell our story. This is exactly what the enemy did not want. He works in secrecy and the darkness of bondage, yet my daughter of strength is speaking truth to me. Tears of joy fell from my eyes and my hands flew up in the air and words of praise flowed from my lips. Jesus promised I would get to know my daughter through Him before I died and He kept His word.

As I'm thanking the Lord, He whispers to my heart and I hear, "Write your book. I will help you. Honor Savannah." Simultaneously, another vision comes into my heart as the Lord's spirit spoke to mine. I saw my daughter at about the age of 16, looking joyful and welcoming me with her smile. She was alone without her angel and I felt a closeness developing between us as the Lord promised. I yearned to ask her the question that has haunted me for two decades.

Jesus has been so good to us and protected us along this journey that I knew this was the time. I asked for her forgiveness and she did not run from me but stayed and warmly greeted me, as though she is waiting for me to be with her. Then, something miraculous happened that I never expected. How could there be anything more miraculous than what has already happened, but Savannah spoke five words, aligned together in a sentence, that I had never heard before. I have read these words in books, used them to prepare documents, and spoke them during casual conversation. I have heard the word 'you' thousands of times and used it as many; sometimes blaming another person or trying to draw attention. The next word in the sentence, 'can', has been part of my vocabulary for years and I never gave it much thought until I heard it from my daughter in a clear confident voice. The third word 'do', is an action word and I'm about getting things done, so I've used this word often throughout my life making and executing plans. The fourth word 'it', is superfluous and is used to direct my attention in a predetermined direction. I've used the fifth word 'Mommy' many times as a little girl trying to get attention, or telling her that I love her. But on this perfect day, I heard these five words, in alignment, one following the other and directed toward me. A human has never released these words from their lips to me. It's something I've always wanted to hear, but years ago, I aborted these words from escaping my daughter's mouth. These words flowed lovingly in my direction and I wanted to capture each one and place them in a vial that only I could hold. I never imagined this kind of love existed in this world. Savannah said, "You can do it Mommy."

The years I spent agonizing over the thought of her hating me dissolved in this moment. Fear and shame enslaved me because rightfully, she should hate me for what I had done to her, but the God I serve does not think the way I do as profoundly stated in the book of Isaiah, "For My thoughts *are* not your thoughts, Nor *are* your ways My ways," says the LORD. "For *as* the heavens are higher than the earth, So are My ways higher than your ways, And My thoughts than your thoughts. (Isaiah 55:8-9 NKJV).

I could feel the warmth of the Lord, like the morning sun rising in the east and settling on my face. He smiled with the love of a parent who sees His two children, where deep pain had been birthed, but He unlocked the gate to healing and brought us together through His power and promise. I have never known this kind of love, nor felt this way before. The Lord made me a promise, kept His word, and presented it to me in a marvelous way that I could never have imagined.

I am grateful after each spirit-filled encounter, thinking this may be the last because Jesus fulfilled His promise, but it never is. When a rock is cast into a still pond, ripples flow in a circular motion, reaching out toward the shore. The shoreline stops the ripples and, in time, the pond is calm. But when Jesus casts a rock of promise into a still pond, the ripples flow from the promise in the same circular motion, gathering witnesses from the north, south, east and west, all reaching for the shoreline that doesn't exist because God's promise has no ending. "Because of the LORD's great love we are not consumed, for his compassions never fail." (Lamentations 3:22 NIV). Jesus' promise is far reaching and contains countless lingering effects that touch others and some we may never know.

The following evening as I prayed, the Lord revealed another vision of Savannah. She's a young woman of 18 years or so and I sense she is patiently awaiting our reunion. Then she does something unexpected and loving. The daughter I thought I would never see, never hold, never love, runs toward me and we embrace. The healing is beyond measure, but Jesus excels at the impossible. I can't explain it, but I know it to be true because I couldn't concoct a story like this. I assumed the door had been slammed shut and locked, but Jesus holds the keys to truth and reconciliation. He lovingly guided His children to full restoration by the stripes on His back and the price He paid for us on Calvary. I think about all He did for me and I can never repay Him, but I try through obedience to His Word. I fail often, but that doesn't mean it's over. I am a witness to Jesus' forgiveness and plan for a future as the prophet Jeremiah spoke of a few thousand years ago. Serving the Lord is light, promise, love, and a way and plan to see those we thought were lost. Actually, nothing ever ends if you believe in Jesus and His Word.

I have a miraculous relationship with my daughter because I turned my eyes to the one who created me. Now, when asked if I have children, I hold my head up with my hair pulled away from my face and say in a strong voice, "I have a daughter, her name is Savannah, and she is with Jesus." What I thought was the end, was truly just the beginning of a repentant heart, a relationship with Jesus Christ, and a promise kept. Only God can turn my most shameful experience into His glory.

CHAPTER THIRTEEN

Healing for Those Who Have

Althought, I had come farther than I could ever imagine, I still carried a light gnawing burden of shame months after receiving God's promise. I didn't feel it all the time, but it was blocking my relationship with Him and my ability to possess complete victory over my testimony and relationship with Savannah.

I accepted the Lord's forgiveness by following His instruction, "Repent therefore and be converted, that your sins may be blotted out, so that times of refreshing may come from the presence of the Lord." (Acts 3:19 NKJV). Yet I still wrestled with unforgiveness for myself. Unforgiveness means having no allowance for error or weakness. As a fallen human being and born of sin, perfection is unattainable. Still, I couldn't reconcile it to my situation because my pride stood in defiance with the lie that I told myself years ago. I was embarrassed by my arrogance, but that's how I felt.

I yearned for understanding and prayed asking Jesus for revelation. I began expanding the impressions I received from Him by studying the root meaning of forgive. In Hebrew, it means to pardon or spare; in Greek it is aphiemi. The prefix **apo** means separation, putting some distance between; **hemi** means to put in motion, send. Therefore, when God forgave me, He actually pardoned, separated, and put distance between me and my sin by sending it away; however, the familiar whispers of condemnation compelled me to pursue it and grab ahold.

In the beginning, I chose to clutch unforgiveness because if I let go, I'd be letting go of my daughter and I'd have nothing left of her. Unforgiveness was the lie that filled the hole in my womb I birthed the day I stumbled out of the abortion clinic. But I met Jesus in my life-saving dream, repented, He filled me with the gift of the Holy Ghost, forgave me, and began re-filling my empty scarred womb with a promise.

Unforgiveness is one of Satan's well-worn tools in his tool box, which prominently displays a Skull and Crossbones warning of fatal death. I looked past the warning sign and invited him into the relationship with Savannah, Jesus, and me when I pursued him and grabbed the deadly hammer of unforgiveness.

When Jesus forgave me for that sin, we put Satan in a prison cell, locked the door and tossed the key. However, prisoners have rights and Satan had access to a phone. I said "yes" when the phone rang and the operator asked if I would accept a collect call from an inmate at the California Department of Corrections. I read some of the familiar mental letters he periodically sent attempting to seductively condemn me. His soft-spoken whispering voice started wooing me and before I knew it, I let him out of prison and he appeared at my doorstep. I didn't recognize that I must have disappointed Jesus. He had painted a masterpiece of my blessed newfound relationship with Savannah. Our relationship is holy and pure and must not be defiled by the one who encouraged the original destruction. When the Lord entrusted Savannah to me 21 years ago, I made the most heinous decision of my life and aborted His plan for her. The Psalmist penned, "Your eyes saw my substance, being yet unformed. And in Your book they all were written, The days fashioned for me, When *as yet there were* none of them." (Psalms 139:16 NKJV).

I was supposed to give birth to Savannah, no matter how sinful, dangerous, or violent her conception, because Jesus had a particular plan for her and I was the birthing instrument. He entrusted me with His glory and I failed miserably. I disrespected Jesus' promise by pursuing unforgiveness and inviting Satan back into the relationship. I understood that unforgiveness of myself is a deadly tool of Satan that manifests in my flesh almost like a third person in a relationship, similar to an affair, which I was keenly aware of and had years of experience in the destruction that it can cause. This revelation freed me to slam the prison door shut, toss the key, revoke letter and phone privileges, and cast him into solitary confinement. The prophet Isaiah said, "For the Lord God will help Me; Therefore I will not be disgraced; Therefore I have set My face like a flint, And I know that I will not be ashamed." (Isaiah 50:7 NKJV). I am forgiven and will not be ashamed because God said so. Jesus loves me therefore, I can love. Jesus forgave me therefore, I can forgive. It's not about me. It's that simple.

If you are reading this book, you have likely been lied to at some point in your life by someone you trusted. Healing from Jesus can only come through faith and trust in Him. Therefore, it is critically important to hear the truth from Him. It's IMPOSSIBLE to heal on our own because we are born of sinful flesh. We must know Him and cultivate an intimate relationship with Him through prayer, fasting, and studying His Word.

If you are not comfortable going to a church, or do not know of one in your area, another option is to contact a local pregnancy resource center and ask about post-abortion counseling https://crisispregnancycentermap.com/. The course I completed with a Christian counselor was a Post-abortive Bible Study for Women, "Forgiven and Set Free," by Linda Cochrane. The counselors and staff ministered to me in a loving, non-judgmental way. I learned who Jesus is, and through the writing exercises I was able to see His goodness, and with time, all the promises that have come true. You were not created to live consumed by shame and guilt. I allowed myself to believe my own lies, and even after committing murder, that still wasn't enough for the father of all lies. Satan wanted me to remain shackled, hurled into a dark dungeon and spend eternity in Hell with him.

No matter what you've done, Jesus will turn it around and use it for His kingdom to help and heal the rest of the flock. Don't ever think you're not worthy because He specializes in people just like us. He didn't come to the hospital and meet with the physicians in the lounge. He came to the intensive care unit where the critically ill lay awaiting His healing. Our brokenness is useful and Jesus is looking for someone just like you and me. "For the Son of man is come to seek and to save that which was lost." (Luke 19:10 KJV). God knows that we were born as sinners and that's why He made a way for us to reconcile ourselves to Him by the work on the Cross and our healing by the stripes on His back.

CHAPTER FOURTEEN

His Stripes

We Christians routinely quote scripture by repeating a series of words as they nonchalantly fall from our lips. Do we sincerely consider the breadth of suffering, humiliation, and physical pain Jesus endured for our sins? I accept the pain and grief I've experienced because I am a sinner, born into sin, and earned my suffering by choosing the wide road that led to destruction. Isaiah 53:5 (KJV) says, "But he was wounded for our transgressions, he was bruised for our iniquities: the chastisement of our peace was upon him; and with his stripes we are healed."

I study the scripture and my eyes were fixed on "his stripes" and I desired a deeper, richer meaning. The English language does not always translate the fullness of words. I yearned to make the scripture more personal and appreciate all Jesus has done for you and me, so I referenced the Hebrew and Greek languages. I understand the scripture to mean that Jesus was slain and put to pain for Rhonda's rebellion, He was beat to pieces, broken and crushed for Rhonda's mischief and sin, the correction and discipline of Rhonda's reconciliation with God was a burden Jesus carried, and with His black and blue marks and wounding thoroughly, made Rhonda spiritually whole and restored Rhonda to God.

During Jesus' time, the Romans were the definitive power and they were a brutal bunch. Crucifixion was a preferred method of capital punishment of foreign captives, rebels and fugitives, and produced a slow death with maximum pain and suffering. During times of war and rebellion, crucifixions numbered in the hundreds or thousands, and the convicted could hang in agony for days before succumbing to death.

The Romans would choose a popular place in clear view to terrorize the population and suppress potential revolt. When Jesus and His disciples, Peter and the sons of Zebedee, James and John, entered the Garden of Gethsemane to pray after the Last Supper, the Gospel of Luke describes the scene as, "And being in agony, He prayed more earnestly. Then His sweat became like great drops of blood falling down to the ground." (Luke 22:44 NKJV). Jesus witnessed the brutality the Romans wielded and knew that extreme torture and deep emotional pain awaited Him, and His flesh recoiled from the Cross, yet the words, "it is finished" must escape His mouth.

Jesus was arrested and tried by the Sanhedrin, a group of rabbis appointed to sit as a tribunal, similar to the United States Supreme Court. They accused Him of blasphemy, or speaking evil, by claiming to be the Messiah. He criticized their corrupt religious system, and His influence grew because His followers witnessed many miracles. They were jealous and spat in His face and punched Him with their fists, while others slapped Him with the palms of their hands. Pontius Pilate, the Roman Governor of Judea, with the zealous endorsement of the Sanhedrin, sentenced Jesus to be crucified by Roman soldiers.

Speculation about how Jesus died continues to be of marked interest. Many articles and books have been written on the subject and theories have been proposed and subsequently rejected. We may never know the exact conditions and source of Jesus' death, but we can be confident that Jesus suffered horribly for many hours and then died a degrading, lonely, excruciating death. He did this willingly, mercifully, in atonement for our sins, and out of profound love for us, and this is an undeniable fact. Therefore, I am providing a perspective from various sources offering a glimpse into the horrific undeserved death of our Holy Savior.

The Romans typically started with scourge or flogging, and only women and Roman senators or soldiers (except in cases of desertion) were exempt. The flagrum was the instrument used to inflict the soul-saving reconciling stripes on Jesus' back.

A flagrum was a short whip made of two or three braided leather thongs or ropes of variable lengths, with small iron balls or sharp pieces of sheep bones tied at intervals, designed to quickly rip the flesh from the body. Sometimes, the Roman scourge contained a hook at the end and was given the terrifying name "scorpion." Jesus would have been stripped of His clothing, wrists shackled and tied to an upright post. He would have been made to stoop, stretching the skin, which made deeper gashes on His back, buttocks, legs, and calves. As the Roman soldiers repeatedly struck Jesus with full force, the iron balls would cause deep contusions, and the leather thongs and sheep bones would cut His skin and subcutaneous tissues, creating quivering ribbons of bleeding flesh. The soldiers would change position periodically and deliver pain-stricken blows from the opposite side. Blows to the upper back and rib area caused rib fractures, severe bruising in the lungs, bleeding in the chest cavity, and possibly partial or complete puncture wounds to the lung causing it to collapse.

Jesus may have vomited, experienced tremors and seizures, and had bouts of fainting. Each excruciating strike would elicit cries of pain. He would be profusely perspiring and exhausted. His flesh mangled and ripped, and would crave water because of the loss of fluid from bleeding and sweating. Tremendous pain and the steady loss of fluids would initiate shock while a slow, steady accumulation of fluid in the injured lungs would make breathing difficult. He would have been growing increasingly weak and light-headed.

According to Jewish law, the number of stripes was forty less one, although, scourging among the Romans was a more severe form of punishment and there was no legal limit to the number of blows, as with the Jews. Deep lacerations, torn flesh, exposed muscles and excessive bleeding would leave Jesus half dead. The Centurion in charge would order the lictor, a Roman civil servant, to halt the scourging when Jesus was near death because He must be kept alive to be brought to public subjugation on the Cross.

The torture Jesus endured is more than most of us could bear, but the chastisement is only beginning. In a most degrading way and in order to mock Jesus, the Roman soldiers placed a purple robe on Him and forced what some believe to be a cap of thorns on His head. The thorns were thrust into His skull and affected the nerves that run through His face, eyes, nose, mouth, and jaw. This would have cut into the large supply of blood vessels in the head area and Jesus would have bled profusely. Trauma to these nerves is said to be the worst pain anyone can experience. They placed a reed in His right hand and bowed down before Him, and mocking Him by saying, "Hail, King of the Jews." They spit on Him and took the reed and struck Him hard on the head. He would have felt unbearable pains across His face and deep into His ears, similar to a hot poker or electrical shock. He would have felt these pains all the way to Calvary and while on the Cross. As He walked and fell on the road to Calvary, He was pushed and shoved, and new pains would have been triggered throughout His body.

How could a humiliated, weakened, beaten, bleeding, mangled mess of a man already suffering from breathing difficulties, as well as hypovolemic and traumatic shock, carry a t-shaped cross that weighed between 175 and 200 pounds? He likely did not.

The cross used in Roman crucifixions consisted of two parts: the upright and the crossbeam. Historic information shows that the upright was already in position at Calvary and Jesus carried the crossbeam. We know that Jesus fell at least three times on the way to Calvary and His condition was extremely serious. Each time He fell, it would have been more difficult to get up. His executioners needed to keep Him alive until the crucifixion and so they made Simon of Cyrene help carry the crossbeam.

Crucifixions were carried out in full view outside the city walls of Jerusalem in a hilly region called Calvary or Golgotha. Roman crosses probably stood about seven feet in height because from a practical point of view, it was easier to lift the crossbeam and victim into position on a shorter cross. Shorter crosses also made it easier for wild animals to finish off the victims. The nails used in crucifixion were made of iron and were about the size of the average screw driver.

By the time Jesus arrived at Calvary, He was in excruciating pain, struggling to breath, and suffering from blood and fluid loss. He was thrown to the ground and forced to lie on His back; the back of quivering ribbons of bleeding flesh. The soldier pressed down on His chest; the chest with broken ribs and possibly a punctured lung. Another held Him down by His legs; legs shredded by the "scorpion," and stretched His arms, one at a time across the crossbeam; arms of bloodied, bruised and torn skin. The pain from the iron nails would have been like having hot pokers driven through His hands, causing bolts of radiating pain up His arms.

The soldiers hoisted Him up by the waist, getting Him to His feet. Every movement, however great or small, sent shock waves throughout His entire body feeling pain from bones to skin. They then bent His knees until His feet were flush and nailed them to the Cross; hammering an iron nail through the top of each foot, severing the plantar nerves. He would have screamed in agony as each swing of the hammer caused a burning, searing pain so severe that the slightest touch or movement felt there is agonizing.

His bent knees further caused cramping and numbness in the calves and thighs. This would force Jesus to arch His back in an attempt to straighten His legs and alleviate the cramping. Finally, raising and mounting the crossbeam to the top of the upright piece would have triggered greater pain.

In the medical sense, Jesus most likely died of traumatic and hypovolemic shock, an opinion that is supported by numerous experts on crucifixion. In the spiritual sense, I think a broken heart contributed to His death.

Jesus is God manifest in the flesh. Therefore, did He foresee how the beautiful likeness of Himself He created in the Garden of Eden would betray Him? As He hung on the Cross battered, bruised and mutilated for our sins, I pray He was looking at those who would turn from their wicked ways and follow the straight road that leads to life. To know you suffered a horrendous death and yet there will be those sheep in His flock who choose to jump the fence in search of greener pastures that don't exist. The pain He endured during the beating came to an end upon His physical death. The disappointment, sadness, and sorrow of our choices to turn from Him must surely break His heart daily, and the unending grief must be worse than the physical beating.

Crucifixion was one of the most horrific and painful methods of death in human history, but have I crucified Jesus in my own personal way? Were my disrespectful words the flagrum that inflicted the numerous lashes on His back? My disobedience to His gentle direction the cap of thorns thrust into His skull? My sinful lifestyle the iron nails driven into His hands and feet? Or worst of all, retrieving the forgiven sin that caused the final blow and broke

His heart? He did all this for me, and I can't forgive what has already been forgiven. This revelation has given me the permission to forgive myself and move forward and help others because I do not want to hurt my Jesus anymore.

He knew what was coming because He journeyed throughout the hills and valleys of Judea since He was a young boy. He probably walked past condemned men hanging on the cross, screaming in pain or eyes being plucked by Carrion crows. His death was not like those languishing on death row in American prisons for decades, most of whom are guilty of the crimes they committed. Jesus was guilty of no crime or sin, and yet He suffered to pay the price for our sins. He did all this for you and me so that we would not walk in shame.

Therefore, if you repent and accept God's forgiveness, don't pick up the flagrum of shame, or the crown of anger, or the nail of pride. Accept the forgiveness of the blood He shed on Calvary and the stripes He endured on His back. Forgive yourself, stay focused on Jesus, and He will use your testimony to help and heal others in the flock.

CHAPTER FIFTEEN

Guidance for Those Who Haven't

An unplanned pregnancy causes great stress and catapults you into a crisis. You hear the tick tock of the clock ticking louder and louder as each day goes by. When I found I was pregnant, I was shocked and desperate for an answer and I acted quickly without thinking. Good decisions are never made in this state of mind. I felt I was backed into a corner and there was only one option available, but that was untrue. There are many resources available to women that I was not aware of. In retrospect, I believe that I would have chosen life if I'd sought guidance at a pregnancy clinic instead of an abortion clinic. I could not see that a year later I'd meet my husband Jimmie, who would have loved Savannah and we could have raised her together. But I was serving Satan, and the years of bad choices pointed me to the wide gate that led to destruction.

Satan wants to kill, steal, and destroy. His voice and my choices blinded my mind and darkened my path so that I only understood and saw what was directly in front of me. Therefore, it is critically important to seek Christian-based counseling in order to remove the blinders and light the path that leads to life. "Satan, who is the god of this world, has blinded the minds of those who don't believe. They are unable to see the glorious light of the Good News. They don't understand this message about the glory of Christ, who is the exact likeness of God." (2 Corinthians 4:4 NLT).

If you are contemplating abortion, I implore you to visit a pregnancy clinic before making a final decision. Many of the counselors and staff at the pregnancy clinic have experienced a similar crisis and are sensitive to your situation. They are humble, demonstrate unconditional love, genuine as they share their personal stories, and empathetic because they have walked in your shoes. They understand that you are scared, face overwhelming pressures, yet you have many strengths. The counselors will help you recognize and identify the power you have over your situation. This is where hope begins. Bear in mind that you make the final decision and they will help and comfort you no matter the outcome.

I think of Savannah often and look forward to the day we can be together in Heaven. Twenty-one years ago, when I made the decision to abort her, I thought life was over for me, and I fully accepted the consequences. It was inconceivable for me to imagine a relationship with Savannah because that's what Satan wanted me to believe. God's love and His Word have given me the freedom and courage to accept His forgiveness. His promises and all He did for me on the Cross gave me the freedom to forgive myself. He fulfills His promises in ways our minds can't imagine. His forgiveness gives me the strength to help others who have made some of the same choices I made. I am here as a witness to what God has done for me and what He can do for you. The Almighty God is my All because He is Mighty.

(The website provides a listing of pregnancy clinics throughout the United States https://crisispregnancycentermap.com/.)

CHAPTER SIXTEEN

Wisdom from Men and Women of God

The military endlessly strategizes, practices, and prepares for battle. Christians must strategize, practice and prepare for the spiritual battle every day, all day, and with more vigor and discipline than a United States Marines' battle cry: Oorah!

Satan will never give up, but he can be rejected and forced to flee. He even tempted our Lord Jesus. "Then Jesus was led up of the Spirit into the wilderness to be tempted of the devil." (Matthew 4:1 KJV). After the tempting, "Then Jesus said to him, 'Away with you, Satan! For it is written, You shall worship the LORD your God, and Him only you shall serve.' Then the devil left Him, and behold, angels came and ministered to Him.'" (Matthew 4:10-11 NKJV).

Most of the time, I am my worst enemy and I can't rebuke or flee from myself. Where do I go? I go to the Word and refresh and cleanse my spirit. I am a greater threat to myself than Satan can ever be because God already defeated him. "Inasmuch then as the children have partaken of flesh and blood, He Himself likewise shared in the same, that through death He might destroy him who had the power of death, that is, the devil." (Hebrews 2:14 NKJV). Satan's power is deception. The only weapon he has is the power we give him when we believe his lies. Our battle with Satan should be against his wily ways, not Satan himself. "Put on the whole armor of God, that ye may be able to stand against the wiles of the devil." (Ephesians 6:11 KJV).

Jesus died a horrific, humiliating death on the Cross for the forgiveness of my sins and restoration to Him. I have accepted His forgiveness and forgiven myself, but I haven't forgotten what I've done. I must remain diligent, keeping my spiritual armor on at all times, rebuking the lies from creeping into my life through the whispers of Satan's voice and my old feelings of shame. Therefore, I use God's ammunition to fight Satan and myself.

I have taken notes from every sermon I have attended these past years and prepared a list of spiritual nuggets to share with you. I pray they help you as they have helped me. These are words imparted, mainly from Pastor Haney, and other men and women who love our Lord Jesus.

ANGELS

- Angels are working *with* me and *for* me. God is not short on help for His people as there are far fewer people than angels.

- When I go to prayer, the angelic world goes to work.

- I am not in a battle against flesh and blood. I serve a God who has given His angels charge around me.

DISOBEDIENCE

- When people reject the truth, there is no telling how far they will go.

- Don't get bitter in my season of suffering. I'm not supposed to lose; I'm supposed to grow.

- Don't allow my physical senses to dictate my spiritual choices.

- People say, "God's not fair." Thank God He's not fair, He's merciful. If He were fair, I'd be in more trouble. MERCY!

- What keeps people from coming to the Lord? Pride!

- The Holy Spirit should be my ego. . .let mine go.

- I can't behave my way into Heaven, but I can misbehave my way into Hell.

- No self-pity; it's the most used tool in Satan's toolbox.

- God chose my tongue because it's the only thing I can't tame – Speaking in Tongues.

- Unbelief will stop what God has planned for me.

- I rob myself of God's blessings every time I define myself by the world.

- If I am failing it's because I am not yielding to the Holy Ghost.

FAITH

- Without faith it is impossible to please God.

- When I'm real and honest with God, then He starts working on me. I give Him something to work with by being honest.

- Jesus never loses faith in me.

- Do not despise the days of small things. Faith is in the little things too. How can God trust me with big things if I'm not willing to do little things – it's about my attitude.

- Even if I don't understand what God is saying, I still need to believe it to be true.

- Faith cometh by hearing, which means to read God's Word aloud.

- If I believe He is true, I must act like He is true. The safest place to be in a storm is with Jesus.

- My confidence is not in my faith, it's in my God.

- There's a difference between doing the best job and the best job "I" can do.

- Stay the Course: Satan can't destroy God's Word because he didn't create it.

- When I don't have confidence in myself, God does.

- If God and I are standing together, we are the majority in every situation.

- There is no high like the Most High God!

FORGIVENESS

- Judas would have been forgiven, but he didn't ask.

- God doesn't compare me with others. Why should I?

- Do something kind for someone else. You can't feel sorry for yourself when you're blessing others.

- You'll know you have the heart of a servant by how you act when people treat you like one.

- I am broken and the Lord says I only use broken things.

OBEDIENCE

- Look My way and obey.

- God expects me to repent and get up again.

- The goal of my life is to please God. Does this please God? I want God to smile at me.

- How powerful Jesus is to me is by how much I submit to Him.

- Believe God's Word above mine.

- I don't have to be perfect. I need to be faithful.

- The supernatural realm can't work with me if I can't keep my tongue.

- Discipleship is giving up what you can't keep to gain what you can't lose.

- If you love Me, obey. Words are cheap if not accompanied by obedience.

- If I *do* what Jesus says, I will *have* what Jesus says.

- Every sin that's not under the blood will be revealed. Repent now and no one will know but me and Jesus.

- We don't have time to play games because He has a plan for us.

- If I want to torment the enemy, do the will of God.

- He can come today. Am I ready?

- God loves those who do wrong and blesses those who do right.

- God does not want to roll the stone away in my life, He wants to resurrect my life.

- Where I spend my time and money is where my heart is.

- It takes more than sincerity – you must obey.

PRAYER

- Don't reason things out in the carnal mind but pray through.

- Seek God's approval in all I do.

- There is nobody too low that the Lord can't reach. Ask the Lord to bless them.

- Tell Jesus all my secrets and not others.

- Prayer is about connecting with my Father.

- If I want effective prayer, I must have a life of holiness – our voice, actions, lifestyle, and dress.

- If I don't have the ability and tell God I can't do it, then He intervenes. But as long as I think I can do it, He won't move. Ask for help!

- We don't need to beg God for anything. We need to believe and God will give me direction.

- If I'm not praying, then I'm fighting the wrong battle.

- How can I have a miracle if I don't have an impossibility. Magnify the Lord with my request. I have to speak prophecy.

- I lack nothing if I know who Jesus is.

- If I touch Jesus I will change.

THE ENEMY

- Television is the voice of Satan.

- The power of Satan is his voice.

- Satan will challenge anyone making a real difference for God.

- I don't go through things so that Satan can destroy me, I go through things so I can help someone else.

- When Satan attacks me – resist and rebuke – tell him to get out.

- Satan trembles when we pray.

- When adversity comes, Satan is trying to stop me from something.

- Satan will use whatever works. If it's hurt feelings, he'll put someone in my path to hurt me.

- Satan doesn't come to pester or aggravate; he comes to destroy.

THE WORD

- My lack of knowledge puts God in a straitjacket. I don't have any fighting power if I don't know the Word which is the sword of the Spirit.

- If I want to be in the perfect will of God, then I must read His Word.

- It's my job to conform to the Word, not the Word to conform to me.

- I was purchased with the precious blood of Jesus, not cheap silver or gold.

- God loves me so much, He traded Jesus' life for me.

- God is watching me always.

- If I say I love God, I must stand up for the truth of His Word.

CHAPTER SEVENTEEN

Letter to My Sweet Savannah

November 13, 2012

To My Dearest Savannah,

Many years ago, I ran away from God our father. I ran so far and so fast that when I turned to see if He was watching me, I couldn't see Him anymore. I was lost. Years later, I became pregnant with you and didn't know what to do. I didn't have God with me anymore. I was scared, alone, foolish, and selfish. So, I gave you to God. He has raised you these past 14 years. He and His angels have done the things I should have done for you.

But a day will come when we will be together. We will walk hand in hand, with our bare feet softly touching the sweet green pasture grass. We will talk and I will show you a hummingbird and tell you that they are the tiniest birds in the world. I will tell you that a hummingbird's heart beats 250 times per minute at rest, and the baby is smaller than a penny. I will watch your eyes get bigger and bigger from wonder. We will stroll and look at the flowers; the poppy, Mommy's favorite. I will tell you how I rode in the foothills near my home and looked out on the hills – the hills that glowed like bright yellow sunshine from all the poppy flowers and how I felt like God was with me on those special days.

We will walk on the beach and we will kick sand in the air. I will chase you from tide pool to tide pool, watching you as you throw you head back and laugh when the tiny hermit crab pokes his head out of his shell and then retreats quickly when he sees you.

I will pick you up and swing you over my shoulder and you will squeal with delight. We will run together down the beach, chasing the seagulls and pelicans. We will lie on our backs on the soft piney bristles amongst the giant redwood trees. We will look up as high as we can see and still not see the top. We will catch the glimpse of a redheaded woodpecker fly by and get to work pecking on a sugar pine nearby. We will be together.

I thank God that you are with Him and you are safe. I thank God for you because you make me want to be the best Christian I can be so that one day, we will be together again. My sweet Savannah, I dream of the day we can be together and walk hand-in-hand, talking, giggling and sharing God's love and wondrous beauty. . .forever.

Love,
Mommy

References

Website: Catholic Insight – The Physical Effects of the Scourging and Crucifixion of Jesus https://catholicinsight.com/the-physical-effects-of-the-scourging-and-crucifixion-of-jesus/

Website: Truth of God – Restoring Original Christianity – For Today! https://www.cbcg.org/scourging-crucifixion.html

Available for Testimony or Speaking Engagement

* * *

To contact Rhonda Lobosco

please email:
RhondaLobosco@comcast.net

connect with on Facebook:
Rhonda Lobosco

www.ingramcontent.com/pod-product-compliance
Lightning Source LLC
LaVergne TN
LVHW041231080426
835508LV00011B/1156